W9-BWP-784

The MLS Project

An Assessment after Sixty Years

Boyd Keith Swigger

THE SCARECROW PRESS, INC.
Lanham • Toronto • Plymouth, UK
2010

Published by Scarecrow Press, Inc.
A wholly owned subsidiary of The Rowman & Littlefield Publishing Group, Inc.
4501 Forbes Boulevard, Suite 200, Lanham, Maryland 20706
http://www.scarecrowpress.com

Estover Road, Plymouth PL6 7PY, United Kingdom

Copyright © 2010 by Boyd Keith Swigger

All rights reserved. No part of this book may be reproduced in any form or by
any electronic or mechanical means, including information storage and retrieval
systems, without written permission from the publisher, except by a reviewer
who may quote passages in a review.

British Library Cataloguing in Publication Information Available

Library of Congress Cataloging-in-Publication Data

Swigger, Boyd Keith, 1943-
  The MLS Project : an assessment after sixty years / Boyd Keith Swigger.
    p. cm.
  Includes bibliographical references and index.
  ISBN 978-0-8108-7703-0 (alk. paper) — ISBN 978-0-8108-7704-7 (ebook)
  1. Library education—United States—Evaluation. 2. Library schools—
Accreditation—United States. 3. Librarians—Certification—United States. I.
Title.
  Z668.S95 2010
  020.711—dc22
                                                        2010010243

∞™ The paper used in this publication meets the minimum requirements of
American National Standard for Information Sciences—Permanence of Paper
for Printed Library Materials, ANSI/NISO Z39.48-1992.

Printed in the United States of America

Contents

Acknowledgments

I am thankful to the librarians and staff of the American Library Association Archives at the University of Illinois Archives in Urbana-Champaign, particularly Mary Miller, for their courtesy and diligence in locating documents relating to the history of the MLS degree. Charles B. Nam, Florida State University, provided a copy of a fugitive paper on status measures and gave me helpful bibliographic leads. Nancy Zimmerman, University of South Carolina, provided copies of materials relating to the development of the ALA policy on personnel utilization as well as tutelage about the workings of the ALA Council. Martin Dillon at Scarecrow Press provided wise advice about matters procedural, stylistic, and substantive. Cindy Potter, Texas Wesleyan University, gave encouragement and served as a wise and patient sounding board throughout my work on this project.

Jessie Swigger, Western Carolina University, and Nathaniel Swigger, Ohio State University, read the manuscript, pointed out errors, and posed appropriate cautionary questions. I am grateful to all for their assistance and their advice. If I did not follow it when I should have, the fault is solely my own.

1

✛

An Overview
of the MLS Project

LIBRARY EDUCATION

In 1951, the American Library Association (ALA) Council approved new standards for accrediting library education programs. The new standards shifted the object of accreditation from the bachelor's degree to the master's degree, making the master's degree in library science (MLS) the professional credential for entry into the profession. Librarians at the time believed this change would transform the practice of librarianship, the nature of library education, and the social standing of librarianship as an occupation.

American librarianship has been animated by a progressive spirit since the late nineteenth century, when librarianship, like other occupations, began to standardize common practices and initiated educational programs that replaced apprenticeship with systematic training.[1] Librarianship operates on the progressive premise that through some careful engineering of policy and practice, librarians can make the world better, for their clients and for themselves. One of the ways professions do that is through control of the education of new professionals. Library education settled into colleges and universities during a period of experimentation with formal educational models from 1877 to 1920. Between 1920 and 1950, librarians and library educators engaged in discussions of the proper nature of library education appropriate to the growth of collections and to the social importance of libraries, producing a series of reports and proposals through their professional literature and conferences. After World War II, librarians, like many other groups, saw opportunities to resume programs of change and reform that had been set aside because of the social disruption caused first by the Great Depression and then by war.

In the postwar period, librarians saw opportunities for growth in library programs and for development of librarianship as a profession. The available supply of skilled librarians was a topic of much concern. The principal debate about library education centered on whether the first professional degree should be a four-year bachelor's degree, a five-year bachelor's degree (the prevailing practice at the time), or a one-year master's degree completed after undergraduate study. Intense discussion in the late 1940s led to a moratorium on accreditation by the Board of Education for Librarianship in 1949, to give the board time to revise the accreditation standards in consultation with professional groups and library schools.[2]

The outcome of all the discussion and revision was what I call "the MLS project," in which the American Library Association redefined the initial credential for professional librarianship. When the Board of Education resumed accreditation in 1953, it was guided by new standards, adopted in 1951, that embodied a commitment by the ALA and library schools to recognize the MLS degree as the first professional credential and to limit ALA accreditation to master's degree programs. The new accreditation was the first step in a process of redefining the term "librarian." After the change, new aspirants to the profession found it imperative to complete an accredited graduate program. Bachelor's degree programs in library science dwindled in number and enrollments. A second step in redefining "librarian" was taken formally in 1970 when the ALA adopted the policy statement "Library Education and Manpower," which distinguished professional work done by librarians—work that called for education in accredited master's degree programs—from nonprofessional work done by support staff.[3] By 1975, 95 percent of academic libraries and nearly 70 percent of public libraries reported that they required a master's degree for employment of new librarians.[4]

However, like many of those who lived their professional lives with it, the MLS project could be nearing retirement. Born in the postwar period amid both great enthusiasm and great uncertainty, and with unvarnished ambitions, the undertaking had a charmed youth followed by a challenging adulthood and then a confused middle age. Now, rather than sitting on the verge of a revered old age, it finds itself confronted with many of the same concerns that it was intended to dispel and facing new challenges in a changed social and technological environment. A look back at the postwar discussions that led to the adoption of the MLS may help us to understand the present situation. The initial debates about library education were framed in terms of what "should" happen and what "would" happen. With the benefit of hindsight, we can assess those arguments of sixty years ago in light of whether the MLS project has accomplished its objectives.

The primary purpose of this book is to recount the reasons ALA enacted the change and to consider its consequences by reviewing relevant data. The questions are: What were librarians' and library educators' arguments for changing the system of library education? What problems were they trying to solve? What were their objectives? Did the change in the structure of library education solve the problems perceived in the late 1940s? Have the objectives been accomplished? What have been some outcomes of the change?

A secondary purpose is to explain librarians' own perspectives on the situation. It is risky to attribute ideas and motives to a whole group, but it is clear that librarians exhibit a strong degree of consistency in attitudes and that they share many perceptions and principles. A key to understanding librarians' view of themselves lies in their broadly recognized model of professionalism. Librarians since Melvil Dewey have held to a simple model in which the traits of professionals comprise a list to which an occupational group like librarians can compare itself. Where their traits do not match the traits in the list, the members of the group attempt to change their traits, confident that in so doing they will achieve recognition and rewards as professionals. This model of professionalism led librarians to expect too much of a change in the credentialing process alone.

Data collected from a variety of sources show that the MLS project has had limited success. Changing the level of the accredited degree did not produce anticipated changes in the substance of library education, nor did it produce the anticipated rewards for graduates of library schools. The project's proponents made professionalism a static concept. Furthermore, librarians, like other professions, could not have foreseen the dramatic changes in the contexts in which they did their work. Those changes, particularly changes in demography and technology, created unexpected circumstances in which the MLS project became an impediment to adapting successfully to new environments.

Librarians individually have invested heavily in their education, as have the various supporters of library schools. Librarianship has been in many ways a successful profession. Libraries as organizations are still socially valued institutions that receive public support. However, librarians as individual professionals have had a mixed experience. While their wages are relatively higher now than in 1951, they still feel insufficiently appreciated. They are still unhappy about their status, and they dislike the stereotypes that define them in the public mind. Certainly one could argue that there are many reasons for librarians' failing to achieve all the goals they set for themselves in the 1940s. That is the point: the profession placed too much confidence in one solution, and that one solution has proved inadequate to the task. Now, the MLS project should be reconsidered in light of what has happened and what has not. Unexamined allegiance to the supposed value of the MLS may be preventing the profession from recognizing alternative opportunities for professional preparation that could be more effective and efficient in producing expert librarians, that could lead to a more inclusive profession, and that could lead to development of better library services and, thereby, to a higher standing for libraries and librarians. The times call for basing professional practices on evidence and for assessing outcomes rather than celebrating hopes.

This book is not a history of library education since 1950. A new history of library education as well as histories of individual schools would be helpful additions to knowledge of the profession. Beverly Lynch has written a brief history, but a full monograph is needed.[5] Rather than attempting such breadth, this book focuses on outcomes assessment, which means presenting data relevant to the goals and consequences of one project within library education. Outcomes assessment has become a popular management tool in libraries and among library funding agencies, such as the Institute of Museum and Library Services. The purpose of an outcomes assessment is to go beyond measurements of resources consumed for some purpose, or how busy people and institutions were, or how dedicated and hard working they were, or how good their intentions were. The purpose of an outcomes assessment is to see if a project accomplished the goals it set for itself in terms of changing lives and social conditions. An outcomes assessment looks at consequences, intended and unintended, to arrive at a conclusion. Having looked at those outcomes, project managers and other stakeholders involved can decide whether the project was or was not worthwhile.

Although this work is not a general history of library education, it does present a historical look at the consequences of the MLS project. When the project was initiated, its creators did not design the kind of systematic assessment plan that contemporary management and funding agencies require of new projects. Consequently, there was no plan for collecting data relating to the outcomes. Indeed, data collection about librarianship and library education has been fragmentary and disorganized. This attempt to explain the results of the MLS project relies on data collected from a variety of sources. None of these data were intended to be used for this particular purpose. The pieces from which the past is made are chosen from the pieces that are available. If the data available were more consistent, more numerous, and more reliable, perhaps a different picture might emerge. I have compiled and stitched together as much pertinent data as possible in order to describe outcomes of the MLS project. There are, admittedly, some holes and ragged edges. Rather than abandon this effort because the data sources were not perfect, I have chosen to "satisfice" in the sense of the term described by Herbert Simon: in the absence of complete data, I have relied on available data in confidence that it is "good enough" for the purpose.[6]

This work is titled *The MLS Project* for several reasons. For most of the last sixty years, the debate centered on the MLS degree, although schools used variant degree titles. For example, my master's diploma from the University of Chicago says "Master of Arts, Graduate Library School"; it specifies the awarding organization but does not say "library science" or "librarianship." Variation still rules. In 1992, the American Library Association, through its *Standards for Accreditation*, renamed the field "library and information studies."[7] As part of the process for revising standards, there had been a long debate in forums sponsored by the Committee on Accreditation about whether to leave the name as "library science" or to change it to either "library and information science" or "library and information studies." The final version of the 1992 standards adopted the latter phrase, which it explained broadly as follows:

> "library and information studies" is understood to be concerned with recordable information and knowledge and the services and technologies to facilitate their management and use. Library and information studies encompasses information and knowledge creation, communication, identification, selection, acquisition, organization and description, storage and retrieval, preservation, analysis, interpretation, evaluation, synthesis, dissemination, and management.[8]

The intent of the 1992 standards was to permit the various graduate schools to present programs as candidates for accreditation with a variety of names, as long as they fell within the definition. The 2008 revision of the *Standards for Accreditation* emphasizes the point more strongly that the name of the field must be construed broadly:

> The phrase "library and information studies" is understood to be concerned with recordable information and knowledge and the services and technologies to facilitate their management and use. Library and information studies encompasses information and knowledge creation, communication, identification, selection, acquisition, organization and description, storage and retrieval, preservation, analysis, interpretation, evaluation, synthesis, dissemination, and management.[9]

Recognized practice within the library education community now is to refer to the field as "library and information studies" and to refer to the standard degree as an MLIS, not an MLS. However, that usage does not appear commonly in the library literature nor in discussions of library education outside the small community of library educators. Furthermore, there is still confusion about what that "IS" stands for. Despite the definition in the accreditation standards as "information studies," many library educators and schools use it to mean "information science." Fifteen schools offer accredited master's degrees in "library and information science," while only five offer accredited master's degrees in "library and information studies." Eight schools still offer the MLS. Together, the library schools' accredited master's degree programs have nearly twenty different titles.[10] The term MLS is still commonly used among librarians, and the degree is held widely. When one refers generically to the MLS degree, librarians know what that means: a first professional credential. One who uses the older term may risk being viewed as antiquated, but given the present contentions about master's programs and what "IS" means, now is a good time to reflect on the profession's experience with the MLS project. I leave to others the task of someday writing an account of "the MLIS project."

Chapter 2 of this work describes the goals of the MLS project, including a discussion of the origins of the project in the postwar environment and the various rationales presented for its undertaking. Chapters 3 through 6 present data, collected from a variety of sources, that relate to the outcomes of the project, both intended and unintended. The outcomes include consideration of status, prestige, and income, as well as impacts on library education and the characteristics of students who became the new generations of librarians. Chapter 7 examines librarians' concept of professionalism and the relationship between that concept and the MLS project. Chapter 8 looks to the future. Rather than offer only a prescription for what should be done, the chapter attempts to provide structure to the various suggestions about what could be done. As librarians consider whether to undertake another major project in the education of new professionals, and thus decide on the future of the profession for another generation, attention to the nature of the arguments made and the evidence considered will be crucial in choosing wisely.

ACCREDITATION

Accreditation is at the heart of the MLS project, so some background information about accreditation may be useful to readers. William K. Selden provides a concise definition that names the elements of accreditation: an agency that does the accrediting; a university or program of study that is accredited; recognition of compliance with the agency's standards; and a set of predetermined qualifications or standards. Selden says, "Basically, accrediting is the process whereby an organization or agency recognizes a college or university or a program of study as having met certain predetermined qualifications or standards."[11]

Accreditation is one of the accomplishments of the progressive movement that began in America in the late nineteenth century. Like other aspects of Progressivism, accreditation is and always has been about control and standards. As Selden states, "Accrediting is a part of the struggle over standards among contending groups."[12] The processes of accrediting began in the 1880s in response to new conditions in higher education. After the Civil War, changes in higher education were part of a broad range of changes in American society resulting from the complementary drives toward industrialization, urbanization, and the development of bureaucratic control systems in many industries and professions. Important changes in higher education included, most notably, an increase in the number of colleges and universities, as well as growth of elective curricula; secularization of college curricula, faculty, and administrators; the founding and rapid growth of land grant colleges; and the importation of the German model of universities devoted to research and to preparation for the learned professions.[13]

The United States had no national education system (and still does not). At the end of the Civil War, in fact, there was little national regulation or standardization of anything, and the absence of a guiding national government hand prompted states and localities to create their own controls in various areas of community life, as they recognized the need to manage a social environment that was changing rapidly and becoming more complex. Higher education accreditation, like many other progressive implementations, began in the states, or in state compacts, as institutions formed partnerships to address common problems. Higher education needed recognized common practices that would lead to predictability in everything from preparation for college to graduation from college. These needs included recognized standards for college preparatory classes that would precede admission to a wide range of institutions, as well as standards for awarding degrees so that one could have a better idea of what a diploma meant.

The immediate common problem for colleges and universities, and those who attended them and supported them, was to define what constituted a legitimate college or university. Educators needed a system for characterizing institutions, so accreditation began as a process that applied to whole schools. That process was carried out on a regional level by associations formed by neighboring colleges and universities. Between 1885 and 1995, the first regional accreditation associations were founded, such as the New England Association of Colleges and Secondary Schools (established in 1885) and the North Central Association of Colleges and Secondary Schools (1895).

Like the higher education community, the various professional communities in the nineteenth and twentieth centuries felt a need for definition and standardization as they moved entrance requirements away from the traditional internship and apprenticeship model into a more formal educational model. Professional accreditation began in the first quarter of the twentieth century, when professional programs of many kinds came to be institutionalized in higher education, and professional associations took seriously the task of defining the characteristics of their particular occupations. The first professional accreditation agencies were in medicine (1906) and law (1921), followed by a host of others. Library education became consolidated in colleges and universities in the 1920s and 1930s. Prior to that, there had been a variety of educational models in place, including college-based training and training programs housed in large libraries. The American Library Association published a list of accredited schools in 1925. Other professions that established accreditation in the 1920s include landscape architecture, music, nursing, optometry, teacher education, and business education.[14]

Professional accreditation may apply to any level of degree program. Different professions have chosen to accredit different degrees, and different professions attach different levels of importance to accreditation. In journalism, for example, bachelor's degrees are accredited, but only about one-fourth of the journalism programs bother to seek accreditation; it is not necessary to graduate from an accredited program to get a job as a journalist.

There are, then, two types of accreditation: institutional accreditation, and professional or specialized accreditation. Institutional accreditation was the first form of accreditation, and it is the function primarily of the regional associations. Institutional accreditation standards and examination processes apply to entire colleges and universities. Some writers about accreditation say the two types are regional accreditation and specialized accreditation. By "regional" accreditation, they mean institutional accreditation, which confuses the accrediting agency with what is accredited. Specialized accreditation, also called professional accreditation, applies to a specific program of study offered by an institution, not to a whole institution.

In some cases, such as journalism, the associations that perform professional accreditation are composed primarily of educators who assess their peers, as does the Accrediting Council on Education in Journalism and Mass Communications. In other cases, as in the case of librarianship, accreditation is carried out by practitioners of the profession who may include professional educators in the process. Although the possibility of an accreditation process carried out by the library educators' association, the Association for Library and Information Science Education (formerly the American Association of Library Schools), has been discussed from time to time, the idea never took hold and there has been no serious effort to move the process of accreditation from the practitioners' association to the educators' association.

ALA accreditation applies to degree programs, not to whole institutions. The ALA accredits only master's programs. It does not accredit undergraduate programs or doctoral programs. It accredits degree programs, not the departments, schools, colleges, or universities in which the programs are administratively housed. The ALA does not accredit individuals. Although the language is cumbersome, the correct form for description of a professionally educated librarian is "X holds a master's degree from a program accredited by ALA." But for simplicity—and thereby creating confusion—people say, "X has an accredited degree" or "X graduated from an accredited library school." Even people who know better often speak loosely about accredited schools, adding to the confusion among those who are not aware of the finer points. One finds the phrase "accredited library schools" throughout the professional literature, on the websites of such professional associations as the Medical Library Association and the American Association of Law Librarians, and even on Web pages of the American Library Association and its divisions, as well as in the ALA publication *American Libraries*.

The actual process of accreditation has been carried out since 1956 by an agency of the ALA, the Committee on Accreditation (COA). Prior to 1956, the ALA agency was the Board of Education for Librarianship. Like other professional associations, the ALA, through its agent COA, has based its approach to accreditation on models developed by the regional associations, whose standards and procedures are all very similar. The regional associations established criteria for membership in the associations. Gradually, and with increasing detail, the eligibility criteria drawn up by the associations evolved into standards.[15] The standards were at first quantitative and prescriptive. In the middle of the twentieth century, accreditation agencies began moving toward accreditation that centered on institutions' missions. By the end of the twentieth century, the assessments of institutions that were candidates for accreditation had shifted from prescriptive statements of required resources to emphasis on outcomes, a focus on accountability, and demonstrations that institutions were effective in accomplishing their goals. A specific model of planning entered the standards, one that called on institutions to involve constituents in planning; organizations were required to demonstrate uses of effectiveness measurements in making decisions. In 1992, after a three-year process of review and consultation by COA, and in accordance with the dominant trend among the regional accrediting agencies, the ALA Council adopted a new set of standards that focused on institutional goals, measures of effectiveness, and consultative planning processes. The 2008 revision of the *Standards* strengthened that emphasis.

NOTES

1. Carl M. White, *A Historical Introduction to Library Education: Problems and Progress to 1951* (Metuchen, N.J.: Scarecrow Press, 1976); Robert H. Wiebe, *The Search for Order, 1877–1920* (New York: Hill and Wang, 1967).

2. American Library Association, Board of Education for Librarianship, 28/50/6, Box 1, letter to library schools, in folder Approval of New Programs in Library Science, American Library Association Archives, University of Illinois, Urbana-Champaign, hereafter cited as ALA Archives.

3. Anthony M. Wilson and Robert Hermanson, "Educating and Training Library Practitioners: A Comparative History with Trends and Recommendations," *Library Trends* 46, no. 3 (1998): 467–504.

4. U.S. Department of Labor, Bureau of Labor Statistics, *Library Manpower: A Study of Demand and Supply*, Bulletin 1852 (Washington, D.C.: U.S. Government Printing Office, 1975).

5. Beverly P. Lynch, "Library Education: Its Past, Its Present, Its Future," *Library Trends* 56, no.4 (2008): 931–53.

6. Herbert A. Simon, *Administrative Behavior: A Study of Decision-Making Processes in Administrative Organizations*, 4th ed. (New York: Free Press, 1997), 119.

7. American Library Association, Committee on Accreditation, *Standards for Accreditation of Master's Programs in Library and Information Studies 1992*, www.ala.org.

8. *Standards for Accreditation of Master's Programs in Library and Information Studies 1992.*

9. American Library Association, Committee on Accreditation, *Standards for Accreditation of Master's Programs in Library and Information Studies, 2008* (Chicago: American Library Association, 2008), 3.

10. Association for Library and Information Science Education, *Library and Information Science Education Statistical Report* (State College, Pa.: Association for Library and Information Science Education, 2005), 238–40.

11. William K. Selden, *Accreditation: A Struggle over Standards in Higher Education* (New York: Harper and Brothers, 1960), 6.

12. Selden, *Accreditation*, 2.

13. Frederick Rudolph, *The American College and University: A History* (Athens: University of Georgia Press, 1990).

14. Selden, *Accreditation*, 60.

15. Barbara Brittingham, "Accreditation in the United States: How Did We Get to Where We Are?" in *Accreditation: Assuring and Enhancing Quality*, ed. Patricia M. O'Brien, *New Directions for Higher Education* 145 (Spring 2009): 7–27, 8.

2

✛

Goals of the MLS Project

THE POSTWAR ENVIRONMENT

In the 1940s, American librarians knew they did not have the same status as other professionals. Although Melvil Dewey in 1876 had declared librarianship a profession, librarians believed they were not receiving the economic and social rewards to which they were entitled, based on the importance of their work to society. They were unhappy with the image popularly held of librarians. And they were concerned about meeting the looming needs for additional librarians to cope with the expected demand for library services in the period following World War II. In 1945, the Carnegie Corporation, which had funded earlier major studies of librarianship, asked Joseph L. Wheeler, retired director of the Enoch Pratt Free Library in Baltimore, to report on the situation of library education. Wheeler found two reasons why recruitment into librarianship was difficult in a strong labor market: the low salaries of librarians and the common requirement for five years of higher education to become a librarian.[1] Recruitment reports from library associations and studies published between 1920 and 1950 showed that barriers to recruitment included not only the extended period of study required and the low salaries but also the low status of librarianship as an occupation, the perceived clerical and routine nature of the work, and the image of librarians as quiet, single females.

In 1946, the American Library Association asked the Carnegie Corporation for funds to study the American public library. The award was made in 1947, and the Public Library Inquiry was conducted by the Social

Science Research Council, directed by Robert Leigh, a political scientist. Data were collected in 1948–1949, including data from a survey of 3,000 librarians. The results of this landmark study were published in 1950 in Leigh's report *The Public Library in the United States*, which described the general situation of public libraries and library education and presented factual data about the conditions of libraries and librarians.[2]

In his discussion of "Library Personnel and Training," Leigh noted that the Public Library Inquiry had begun with the assumption that librarianship was a profession, but as the researchers discovered, "Two-thirds of work was found to be nonprofessional, either technical or clerical or maintenance" while the other third "consisted of staff activities of an administrative or specialized character calling for some degree of personal judgment and breadth or depth of intellectual background."[3] Leigh observed that many libraries were small, so librarians were called on to do technical, clerical, and maintenance tasks along with their professional work. Even librarians working in larger libraries were not recognized as professionals because so many of them combined professional work with nonprofessional work.

Not only was their work largely nonprofessional, but also the majority of librarians did not meet the minimum educational standard for professional positions set by librarians themselves. The Inquiry found that only 58 percent of the library personnel designated as professional by librarians had earned bachelor's degrees, while only 40 percent had a full year of professional training. The professional training did not fit the mold of professions generally. Comparing professions and other occupational groups, Leigh said, "The distinction is that a profession possesses specialized, communicable techniques based upon: (1) prolonged intellectual training; (2) a content of training that includes generalizations or principles; (3) the application of the principles in concrete professional practice, a complex process requiring the exercise of disciplined, individual judgment." Training for librarianship, however, was different from training for other professions because librarians were expected to have command of knowledge in many areas: "Certainly, some of the specialized library techniques are based upon prolonged intellectual training. But the intellectual content of the training consists of acquaintance with the whole range of knowledge rather than the one or two fields of science or learning usually underlying other professions. Thus, it is frequently said that librarianship is a specialization in generalism."[4]

Leigh concluded that librarianship is "a skilled occupation on its way to becoming an organized profession." Salaries for library work were low compared to those for other occupations. In 1948, the salary recommended by the ALA for beginning professional librarians was $2,800 per year. The actual median salary for a librarian with an average of seventeen years of service was $2,700. Leigh noted that the average factory worker earned $3,000 per year.[5] In equivalent 2008 dollars, based on the Consumer Price Index, the median librarian salary would be $24,141 while the factory worker salary would be $26,823.[6]

Librarians looked at what they could control and saw that they did have great influence on education for librarianship. So they centered their efforts on alterations in the structure of library education as a means to effect changes in status, income, and the work itself. In 1946, formal library education comprised three types of programs, each accredited by the ALA Board of Education for Librarianship. Type I schools required a bachelor's degree for admission to the professional curriculum, which led to a master's degree. Type II schools required a bachelor's degree and gave a one-year course culminating in another, fifth-year bachelor's degree. Type III schools did not require a bachelor's degree or four years of college.[7] These three types of schools were built on a common assumption that training for the practice of librarianship rested on acquisition of a set of technical skills. There was disagreement, however, about whether effective application of those skills also required a substantial education in the arts and sciences. In the five-year programs, the fifth year was the time in which library skills were added to a bachelor's level education in subjects other than librarianship.

In 1948, there were 36 accredited programs. The Public Library Inquiry found that 13 library schools offered a year of training as part of a bachelor's degree; 23 offered a year of training after completion of bachelor's work and then awarded a baccalaureate degree at the end of the five years; 4 of those 23 awarded a master's degree for a second year of post-baccalaureate study (a total of six years); and 1 awarded both master's and doctoral degrees. The library schools typically had the smallest faculty and enrollments among professional schools in their institutions. The curricula, regardless of degree level, focused on five common core areas: cataloging and classification, bibliography and reference, book selection, library administration, and the history of libraries, books, and printing.[8]

Attention focused on what to do about the five-year degree (Type II schools). There was widespread concern that continuing five-year bachelor's degree programs made recruitment to librarianship difficult.[9] The question posed was whether library education should be extended "downward" into the undergraduate program, to allow completion of both library training and a subject degree in four years, or whether successful completion of the fifth year should result in a master's degree. Each side in the debate advanced its arguments in terms of practical consequences.

Proponents of change advocated a variety of approaches, and stated their proposals with varying degrees of supporting argument. Some of the proponents merely argued what should be done; others based their proposals on specific assumptions or evidentiary claims. Like most social policy debates, the one about library education was not a clear juxtaposition of contrasting premises, arguments, and evidence arrayed against one another in a neat dialectic. Rather, the discussion was more historical than logical. Research played only a small part, at best. Lowell Martin, dean of the Graduate School of Library Service at Rutgers University, observed that in the 1930s there were many articles and books about library education, but "very few gained depth and significance by virtue of research" and the same was true of discussion in the 1940s: "The next decade saw no diminution of writing about library education, nor very little increase in research into it, even though the schools were moving toward a major modification in programs."[10] Lester Asheim put it baldly in 1957 when he said of the movement of library education to the master's degree, "The purpose of the change is, of course, to advance the professional status of library education."[11] In the exchanges of opinion, as Martin wrote, "research directly on library education—its content, method, or results—seems to have played only a minor role. At most it aided a few compelling judgments that had a discernible influence."[12]

COMMON GOALS AND PRINCIPLES

The parties in the discussion about library education each brought their own interests, backgrounds, and preferences to the conversation. The situation was one in which various proposals were set forth, which sometimes complemented and sometimes contradicted each other in their specific parts. In this tangle, however, one can discern common threads, including some common principles and premises. The shared goals of the reformers of library education ultimately became the goals of the MLS project.

Recruitment: The quantity of librarians had been a concern since the 1930s. The financial constraints on libraries during the Depression limited the positions available for librarians, and enrollment in library schools had declined. During World War II and immediately after, improved economic conditions and increasing population led librarians to conclude that the time was ripe for increasing the number of librarians. The difficulties concerning recruitment included competition from other academic programs leading to occupations that paid better, had greater prestige, and did not require as many years of higher education. The MLS project would address the problem by granting a higher degree for the same amount of time in school and by awarding a higher and thus more prestigious degree. Furthermore, the mere fact that graduate study was required would lead to two outcomes: more academically qualified students would apply, and they would come to library education having completed a liberal arts and sciences education.

Differentiation between undergraduate and graduate program content: One of the perceived problems with the accreditation of undergraduate degrees was that it was unclear whether a four-year BLS degree program had or had not prepared students at the same level as a five-year BLS degree program. There was confusion about whether the curricula taught fundamental skills and techniques necessary to work in a library or whether the programs were presenting higher-level content that led to expertise that differentiated librarians from library assistants. The MLS project would address that problem because schools would not offer basic skills courses for graduate credit.

A stronger intellectual base for librarianship: Librarians wanted to make it clear—and to make it so—that librarianship comprised mastery of intellectual concepts which professionals applied to intellectual problems, and to dispel notions that librarianship was merely a set of operational routines that were mostly clerical. By locating library education in graduate programs, library science would be seen as the equal of other graduate programs. Library educators teaching at the graduate level would elevate the content of their curricula to make it consistent with the higher degree level.

Differentiation between professional librarians and other persons employed in libraries: Librarians were aware that the public thought all people who worked in a library performed the same work and had the same educational background. The public face of librarianship, the public points of contact and interaction with library staff, typically centered on the least intellectual of tasks—checking out books, for instance. The more intellectual tasks, such as assessing works that were candidates for selection or cataloging books once acquired, were invisible to library patrons, and sometimes to those responsible for hiring librarians. A formal differentiation based on education credentials would help to distinguish between the professional librarians and library assistants. This differentiation by degree would lead to different work assignments, different salaries, and different degrees of prestige.

Increased status, prestige, and income for librarians: Librarians wanted to be more successful. They wanted more money. They wanted higher status and prestige within their communities and among the professions at large. They wanted more respect. These are common human desires, so it is no surprise that they were so forcibly stated in the discussions about changes needed. Librarians, contrary to the stereotype and to some degree in an irritated response to it, were not shy about asserting that they deserved more than society had so far granted them.

Notably absent from most of the discussions was explicit attention to improvement in the quality of library services. Better library service was not a prominent goal, partly because librarians were already confident that they were providing good service. They just wanted the resources that would enable them to continue to do so, and the recognition they believed they deserved for doing it. Indeed, there was little discussion of problems relating to services other than a shortage of staff and a shortage of funds for libraries. Librarians took it for granted that they were doing good work, while arguing that they could do better work if they had higher status, higher salaries, and more advanced educational degrees. Librarians did not believe their work needed substantial revision or correction, but they were convinced that the public failed to recognize their importance. That concern pervaded discussion of the need for changes in library education.

ARGUMENTS AND ASSUMPTIONS

The arguments made for change rested on intertwined assumptions and assertions more than on logical steps with accompanying evidence. The commentators on library education were more notable for their faith in their assertions and their confidence in the outcomes of their proposals than they were for systematic analysis of the situation. In the discussions at the time, there was not an orderly process of planning such as the current ALA *Standards for Accreditation* requires of library educators. Some of the elements missing from those discussions, which would be expected under the present model, were needs analyses of library patrons and library school students, the personnel needs of libraries as organizations, the interests and needs of sponsoring institutions such as universities, the competencies required of new librarians and of librarians at various stages of their careers, or constituent inputs on policies and practices. The point is not to hold planners at a different moment in history to the present criteria for planning, but rather to state that the planning process at the time was not as rigorous as academic and professional planning has become. Rather than a rigorous planning process, those involved in the discussions then presented to one another a set of rhetorical reactions to some perceived problems.

The biggest question was whether to focus on graduate or undergraduate education for librarians. Joseph Wheeler, reporting to the Board of Education for Librarianship on organizations' responses to his 1946 study *Progress and Problems in Education for Librarianship*, said that the argument about graduate versus undergraduate education centered on three factors: which level of education would be best for recruiting new librarians;

which level would lead to better salaries for librarians; and which level would lead to enhanced status and recognition of librarianship as a profession.[13] He reported that generally school librarians favored undergraduate programs, but other types of librarians favored graduate programs.[14] Importantly, Wheeler saw correctly that the level of instruction was not argued as a question of intellectual complexity. It was argued as a matter of strategies for librarians to be successful. The arguments made by those who took positions on the question of undergraduate versus graduate education reflected Wheeling's finding.

Anita Hostetter, secretary to the Board of Education for Librarianship, advocated an extended undergraduate program. Prior to ALA Midwinter 1947, she developed a draft statement for the board to consider, in which she wrote, "conditions in the field of librarianship are emphasizing the desirability, if not the actual necessity, of introducing a basic program of library science in the undergraduate years."[15] Ralph Munn, chair of the board, did not disagree but was concerned about the process for making a decision. He advised Hostetter to take a more moderate position, and to let the library schools rather than the board take the lead in making a decision on the matter.[16] The board discussed the draft at Midwinter and approved a statement on January 31, 1947, that endorsed expansion of library education within undergraduate programs.[17]

The statement, published in the *ALA Bulletin*, said, "The proposal that the initial professional training for library work be introduced more generally within the undergraduate college programs appears to be gaining favor in the library profession."[18] The statement cited four "advantages" of an undergraduate program:

1. It will presumably provide the preparation needed for library positions which do not require the completion of four years of college plus the present curriculum of one year offered by library schools.
2. By being placed in the undergraduate college, it will become a means of recruiting young people who are often discouraged by the prospect of spending five years in preparation for library work.
3. It can be so planned and scheduled in relation to courses in subject fields that the total undergraduate education of the prospective librarian will be directed toward professional library service.
4. As a program required of all librarians, it will provide a base for a graduate curriculum in the fifth college year which can justifiably lead to a master's degree.

Some library educators agreed with the board's statement. Wharton Miller, director of the Syracuse University Library School, proposed a three-level approach: a liberal arts foundation; a core of library studies in the senior year, which he saw as sufficient for employment; and potential elaboration or specialization at the graduate level. Miller distinguished between a first professional credential (the bachelor's degree in his scheme) and a final professional degree. His rationale supported the board statement on undergraduate programs and added some additional arguments. Syracuse proposed an extended undergraduate program for the following reasons:

- One year can present all the education to meet the needs of the many and varied openings for beginners.
- There is a basic core of knowledge common to every library job, but it can be covered in one half a year.
- A postgraduate program delays entering the profession too long.
- About half of most programs at the fifth year (Type II) are not of graduate quality.
- Educators think in terms of amount of time that is available, not in terms of how much time it takes to cover content.
- Study of the liberal arts for four years is good for some but not for all: "the requirement of the bachelor's degree serves no better purpose, for all our rationalization, than to make a convenient device for selecting or rejecting students."[19]

Miller said that although a graduate degree might help in advancing the status of librarians among other professionals, it was questionable whether the intellectual content of library education was in fact material appropriate to graduate-level instruction.

Nathaniel Stewart, a proponent of replacing the fifth-year program with a one-year master's degree, also had such qualms but nonetheless supported moving library education to the graduate level. He suggested that faculty would develop graduate-level content if they had graduate-level classes to teach. "Despite the wealth of literature on library education, there is much to be done in arriving at a discipline of studies which can be strongly defended as graduate studies," Stewart admitted, but he said that library education should be moved to the graduate level anyway because having graduate programs would provide the opportunity "to develop a genuine graduate curriculum." Stewart also argued that there were practical reasons for favoring a graduate program over an extended undergraduate program. If undergraduate programs more integrated with the four-year bachelor's degree were perceived as terminal degrees for librarianship, he said, many people would halt their professional training after receiving a BS, and thus graduate with a "subprofessional outlook and temperament." Librarianship, he said, already had too many technicians.[20]

The University of Washington library school faculty also presented an argument against integrating library education into the undergraduate degree. Robert Gitler wrote an open letter to the editor of the *ALA Bulletin* on behalf of the faculty of the University of Washington School of Librarianship in response to the board's statement on undergraduate programs. Gitler and his colleagues opposed further development of the undergraduate library science degree because they believed the existence of widespread undergraduate programs would result in a cheap labor market and lead to "a depreciation of professional currency," revealing a belief that use of the credentialing process to restrict the supply of librarians was a legitimate tactic. They also sought closer parallels to recognized professions, which they said did not have easy undergraduate routes for entry. And they argued that either at the undergraduate or master's level, the educational program would still require five years to achieve a true professional degree. They also made an argument in terms of liberal education, saying that further elaboration of undergraduate library science courses would cause curtailment of other undergraduate courses, so the undergraduate library science degree would interfere with broad undergraduate education. "Pursuing a curriculum of library science for library science itself, although not purposeless, is of doubtful value. Therefore, the most logical undergraduate training for librarianship is not librarianship itself but rather a broad cultural (humanistic) or intensive subject preparation prior to entering the professional curriculum of librarianship."[21]

Alternatives to the existing system for library education were discussed at the library school deans and directors Conference on Education for Librarianship, held at the University of Illinois in October 1947. In her summary of the conference, Anita Hostetter saw no agreement on two major issues: how to draw a distinction between vocational education and academic education, and whether the curriculum for librarianship should be located in undergraduate or graduate programs. In a memorandum to board members, she summarized the arguments concerning degree location. The arguments for locating professional curriculum in undergraduate programs were that such placement has recruiting value; that it is sound policy to begin professional study early in the education scheme; and that students can more easily drop out to take jobs and reenter later, if necessary. The arguments for the graduate programs were that a graduate program makes the best use of a five-year plan of study; that professional education at the graduate level is geared to students of "greater intellectual maturity"; and that the master's degree can be obtained in the same amount of time as a five-year bachelor's program.[22] Not everyone saw the conference as Hostetter did. An unsigned report on the conference observed, "Here, it is quite apparent that there is an inclination to abandon the fifth-year bachelor's degree and to give a master's degree for the same period of time."[23]

Hostetter did see some areas of broad agreement. She wrote to the board that there was a consensus that library schools were moving more toward five-year bachelor's programs or master's programs, that the whole higher education experience should be seen as part of a student's professional preparation, and that there was a need to relate the content of undergraduate education to the requirements for definite types of library work.[24] Hostetter said that levels of complexity of library work could be articulated with educational levels. Undergraduate training would be for technicians. Graduate degrees would be for those preparing for library management.

Ultimately, the winning arguments were those that said moving library education to the graduate level would lead to higher status and income for librarians and recognition that librarians were peers with other professionals. The opinion that prevailed was that achievement of professional status, more successful recruitment, and better salaries for librarians would result from moving library education to the master's level. Librarians saw the MLS project as a means to alter their social standing. They believed it would alter potential recruits' perceptions of the value of library education by awarding a master's degree for five years of study. Seeing that librarians held graduate degrees, society would pay librarians more. As Everett C. Hughes observed, "It is part of the American ideology that the longer one has to go to school for a profession, the higher that profession's standing."[25] By making distinctions among those who worked in libraries, the MLS project would change public perceptions of librarians, and thus their prestige, by separating those who do professional work from those who do technical and clerical work. Librarians set out to change their social status and prestige, to increase their incomes, and to make the profession more attractive as a career choice.

SUMMARY

The goals of the MLS project were:

- Increased status, prestige, and income for librarians.
- More successful recruitment to the profession in terms of numbers and qualities of applicants to programs.
- A recognized distinction between training in library skills and education in principles, theory, and management.
- Development of a stronger intellectual base for librarianship.

- Differentiation between professional librarians and other persons employed in libraries.

Librarians believed that some of the most defining and influential characteristics and features of their occupation were dependent on the MLS project. These characteristics and features can be treated as variables about which data are available in a wide variety of sociological studies and statistical reports. Accomplishing changes in all these variables together placed a heavy burden on one instrument, the master's degree in librarianship. Nonetheless, the supporters of the MLS project placed great confidence on the outcomes that they believed would accrue from a new professional credential. Did the project have the anticipated outcomes?

NOTES

1. Joseph L. Wheeler, *Progress and Problems in Education for Librarianship* (New York: Carnegie Corporation, 1946).
2. Robert D. Leigh, *The Public Library in the United States: The General Report of the Public Library Inquiry* (New York: Columbia University Press, 1950).
3. Leigh, *The Public Library*, 186.
4. Leigh, *The Public Library*, 218, 190.
5. Leigh, *The Public Library*, 192, 195.
6. Calculated using the CPI dollar value converter at www.measuringworth .com/uscompare/.
7. Wheeler, *Progress and Problems in Education for Librarianship*, 10.
8. Leigh, *The Public Library*, chap. 14.
9. See, for example, Agnes Lytton Reagan, *A Study of Factors Influencing College Students to Become Librarians*, ACRL Monographs 21 (Chicago: Association of College and Research Libraries, 1958).
10. Lowell A. Martin, "Research in Education for Librarianship," *Library Trends* 6, no. 2 (1957): 207–18, 211.
11. Lester Asheim, "Education for Librarianship," *Library Quarterly* 25, no. 1 (1955): 76–90, 82.
12. Martin, "Research in Education for Librarianship," 213.
13. Wheeler, *Progress and Problems in Education for Librarianship.*
14. Board of Education for Librarianship, 28/50/6, Box 6, folder Wheeler Committee, ALA Archives.
15. Board of Education for Librarianship, 28/50/6, Box 5, folder Statement on Undergraduate Courses in Library Science, 1946–47, ALA Archives.
16. Board of Education for Librarianship, 28/50/6, Box 5, folder Statement on Undergraduate Courses in Library Science, 1946–47, letter from Ralph Munn to Anita Hostetter, ALA Archives.

17. Board of Education for Librarianship, "Undergraduate Courses in Library Science: A Statement on Undergraduate Courses by the Board of Education for Librarianship," *ALA Bulletin* 41, no. 3 (1947): 70.

18. Board of Education for Librarianship, "Undergraduate Courses in Library Science," 70.

19. Board of Education for Librarianship, 28/50/3, Box 1, folder Board of Education for Librarianship Book September 1947–December 1948, letter from Wharton Miller, Director of Library School, Syracuse University, to Miss Hostetter, August 4, 1947, ALA Archives.

20. Board of Education for Librarianship, 28/50/3, Box 1, folder Board of Education for Librarianship Book May 1945–August 1947, ALA Archives.

21. Board of Education for Librarianship, 28/50/6, Box 5, folder Statement on Undergraduate Courses in Library Science, Robert Gitler letter April 1, 1947, ALA Archives.

22. Board of Education for Librarianship, 28/50/6, Box 1, file Experimental Programs, Approval of, ALA Archives.

23. University of Illinois Alumni Newsletter, 1948, 9–10, Board of Education for Librarianship, 28/50/6, Box 1, file Experimental Programs, ALA Archives.

24. Board of Education for Librarianship, 28/50/6, Box 1, file Experimental Programs, ALA Archives.

25. Everett C. Hughes, "Introduction," in *Education for the Professions of Medicine, Law, Theology, and Social Welfare: A Report Prepared for the Carnegie Commission on Higher Education*, ed. Everett C. Hughes, Barrie Thorne, Agonstino M. DeBaggis, Arnold Gurin, and David Williams (New York: McGraw Hill, 1973), 2.

3

+

Librarians' Standing: Status, Prestige, and Income

The MLS project sought to improve librarians' standing in society in terms of their status, prestige, and income. The goal of improved standing involved an enhancement of rewards and the regard in which society holds librarians, as well as improved standing in relation to particular groups, specifically the library workers not regarded as real librarians and the professionals among whom they sought to be regarded as peers. This chapter looks at the status, prestige, and income of librarians compared to the standings of those engaged in professions that librarianship claims as peers. In the early part of the twentieth century, the major traditional professions were the clergy, medicine, and law.[1] Librarians saw themselves as close to the latter. As Pierce Butler, a professor at the University of Chicago Graduate Library School, put it in 1951, "we all do believe that librarianship is a profession. We have long since come to feel that it belongs in the same category as do such vocations as medicine, law, and engineering."[2] Over the years, librarians have compared themselves to other occupational groups as well, primarily in fields of education. In the popular mind, and among librarians themselves, teaching is often referred to as the profession with which librarianship shares values and functions. School librarians consider themselves teachers, and many states require teacher certification prior to certification as a librarian.[3] Academic librarians view the library as an instructional center and consider librarians functional peers of faculty.[4] Many public librarians see a vital role for librarians in teaching information literacy, and in the public mind the most important role of the public library is educational.[5] After about 1970, some librarians began identifying their occupation as an

23

"information profession" and claimed functional similarity to workers in the computer sciences.

STATUS

The status of librarianship in the 1940s is unclear because few outside the field paid much attention to it. Librarians still do not attract much attention: a Harris poll of prestigious occupations in 2006 did not ask about librarians.[6] A 1947 study of the relative standing of jobs and occupations, conducted by the National Opinion Research Center (NORC), did not include librarianship among the ninety occupations for which data were gathered.[7] As shown in table 3.1, however, the 1947 survey did present useful information about how people assess occupational status, finding that high income is the most important criterion for rating an occupation as having "excellent standing." Second in importance was whether a job "serves humanity" and is "essential." Third in importance, tied with "the job carries social prestige," was "preparation [that] requires much education, hard work, and money." In seeking status through extended education, librarians might have found hope in such a finding because "preparation," unlike a salary, is a variable over which an aspirant to status can have some control. Control of credentials and admission to the profession is the source of power for professions, such as librarianship, which conduct their practice within organizations and whose expertise

Table 3.1.   1947 Survey of Evaluations of Jobs and Occupations

Question: "When you say that certain jobs have 'excellent standing,' what do you think is the one main thing about such jobs that gives this standing?"

Source of Standing	% Citing
The job pays so well	18
It serves humanity; it is an essential job	16
Preparation requires much education, hard work, and money	14
The job carries social prestige	14
It requires high moral standards, honesty, responsibility	9
It requires intelligence and ability	9
It provides security, steady work	5
The job has a good future; the field is not overcrowded	3
The job is pleasant, safe, and easy	2
It affords maximum chance for initiative and freedom	0
Miscellaneous answers, don't know, no answer	10

Source: National Opinion Research Center, "Jobs and Occupations: A Popular Evaluation," *Opinion News,* September 1, 1947.

is applied through bureaucracies and standardized solutions to specific problems.[8]

Librarians tackled a difficult task in attempting to change their social standing. Status depends on education and income, and although librarians have some control over the educational requirements for their occupation, they have much less control over their income. The criteria of service and essential value to humanity that emerged in the NORC survey imply both motives and judgment. The implied motive is the motive to serve. The judgment implied is about what functions are essential to society. Such a judgment rests on principles ranging from the philosophical to the religious to the intensely personal; these are topics about which librarians may have opinions and arguments, but those are not universally known or shared. Prestige is a matter of perception, awarded as an act of perception. Prestige cannot simply be claimed by those who seek it. A group such as the American Library Association can attempt to shape how the public perceives its members, through marketing and public relations, but ultimately the perception is shaped by many factors, most of which are beyond the group's control.

In measuring the status or prestige of an occupation, it is important to note that sociologists are concerned with the standing of occupations themselves and not of the persons who happen to work in a particular occupation at a given moment. Furthermore, sociologists distinguish between occupational status and prestige and thus measure each somewhat differently. Status can be measured by reference to objective characteristics, whereas prestige depends on opinions that society holds about a particular occupation. Charles Nam and Monica Boyd explain the difference between studies of social standing that are based on perceptions and those that are based on objective characteristics such as education and income:

> If prestige is what we intend to measure, and operational measures of it relate to judgments made by persons concerning the "social standing" of other persons or the positions they hold, as is the case with the vast majority of occupational scales found in the research literature, then the resulting indicators must be interpreted as relating to status attributes such as prestige, respect, honor, and reputation. If, on the other hand, the intention is to measure social class or socioeconomic level, and operational measures of it are reported objective characteristics such as education and income, then the resulting data should be interpreted as indicating the level of living of those being studied.[9]

This book uses the term "status" as Nam used it in a number of studies over several decades, as a measure of relative standing among occupations based on the objective measures of income and education. Librarians' status in the last half of the twentieth century did increase, partly because the definition of status uses educational level as one component of the measurement. By requiring more education, and by defining librarians as only those persons who had the required education, librarians in effect pushed their own status higher, which was one of the goals of the MLS project. If all other occupations had done the same thing, then the status of librarians would not have changed, but not all of the others did, so relative to many occupations, the status of librarianship rose.

THE STATUS OF LIBRARIANSHIP AMONG PROFESSIONS

Charles Nam and his associates have measured occupation status based on education and income for each of the decennial censuses since 1950. The method used is detailed by Nam and Mary Powers, and the scores it creates are called Nam-Powers scores.[10] The same method has been used to calculate occupational status scores for the occupations listed in the last six censuses. The scores are relative scores for occupations within each census year. In addition to its repeated use, a strength of the occupational status score method is that it is interpretable. A score indicates "the approximate percentage of persons in the experienced civilian labor force who are in occupations having combined levels of education and income lower than the given occupation."[11] That is, the score of 64 for librarians in 1950 indicates that librarians had higher combined levels of education and income than approximately 64 percent of the labor force; the score of 82 in 2000 indicates that librarians' levels of education and income exceeded those of 82 percent of the population. Librarians' status among all occupations rose between 1950 and 2000.

However, the MLS project set forth not only to increase the status of librarianship broadly speaking but also to establish a place among other professions as a peer. That effort has been less successful. Comparison of the status scores shows that librarians have moved ahead only in comparison to the clergy. In 1950, librarians had lower status than physicians, lawyers, clergy, and teachers. In 2000, librarians had lower status than physicians, lawyers, teachers, and computer programmers and systems analysts (the latter two titles were not used in 1950). While they have done well in comparison to all occupations and in comparison to the status of other library workers who are not considered librarians, librarians have not excelled in status compared to the professionals they think of as their peers. Table 3.2 compares occupational status scores of librarians and library assistants to a select group of professions over the period 1950 to 2000.

While librarians did not excel in status, they did make some gains in relative standing. Educators, to whom librarians are often compared, saw

Table 3.2.   Occupational Status Scores by Census

Occupation	1950	1960	1970	1980	1990	2000
Librarian	64	72	75	72	75	82
Physician	99	99	99	100	99	99
Lawyer	98	99	99	99	99	99
Clergy	67	65	77	76	80	75
Engineer	96	95	98	95	95	94
College teacher	96	95	91	93	91	86
Elementary teacher, public school	89	85	80	78	84	83
Secondary teacher, public school	89	85	86	82	89	86
Computer programmer			89	84	89	90
Computer systems analyst			93	94	94	89
Library assistant/technician	50	47	44	38	39	22

Note: Teachers are grouped together in the report of status scores for 1950 and 1960; College teachers are grouped with college presidents in the report of status scores for 1950 and 1960; For 1970, 1980, 1990, and 2000, college teachers are reported by discipline; the score reported here is an average; the scores for engineers are averages across types of engineering.

Sources: for 1950 and 1960, Charles B. Nam and Mary G. Powers, "Changes in the Relative Status Level of Workers in the United States, 1950–1960," *Social Forces* 47, no. 2 (1968): 158–70; for 1970, Charles B. Nam and Mary G. Powers, *The Socioeconomic Approach to Status Measurement* (Houston, Tex.: Cap and Gown, 1983); for 1980, Charles B. Nam and E. Walter Terrie, "1980 Based Nam-Powers Occupational Status Scores," Working Paper 88–49 (Tallahassee: Center for the Study of Population, Florida State University, 1988); for 1990, Charles B. Nam, "1990 Occupational Status Scores," data file provided by Dr. Nam, May 2, 2007; for 2000, Charles B. Nam and Monica Boyd, "Occupational Status in 2000: Over a Century of Census-Based Measurement," *Population Research and Policy Review* 23 (2004): 327–58.

their scores decline over the fifty-year period, while librarians' status scores increased, so the relative improvement for librarians is due both to librarians' success and to teachers' difficulties. But still librarians lag behind educators in occupational status. Librarians' status was lower than the status of those in the computer-related professions from the time data on computer professions were first reported.

One would expect to see an increase in the relative status of librarians after 1950 because the MLS requirement for librarians would gradually lead to replacement of the librarians in place in 1950 with librarians who entered the profession after 1950 who had earned master's degrees as their initial credentials. The initiation of the MLS project accounts for the higher score levels in 1960 and 1970 compared to 1950. The increase in the score from 1990 to 2000 probably reflects an increase in salaries of librarians in the boom period of the late 1990s. One must be cautious in comparing scores across census intervals; these scores are most useful in assessing relative status of professions at the time of a particular census, but decade to decade comparisons for the same occupational group may be misleading because there is no absolute standard for status. Status is always relative. The fact that one's percentile score may change, on any scale, does not necessarily mean that one is improving or declining; it may simply mean that those to whom one is compared are changing. Higher percentile scores of librarians may be due to positive factors that benefited librarianship or to unrelated factors that had a negative influence on other professions. The progress of the enormous Baby Boom generation through its life cycle clearly influenced the teaching professions that served it most directly, creating a shortage of teachers in the boomers' early years and a surplus after they had moved through the schools.

These occupational status scores show that the MLS project did accomplish one of its major goals, which was to establish a distinction between librarians and other library workers such as library assistants or technicians or clerks (various names are used for library assistants in the census classifications 1950–2000). Librarians wanted to distinguish themselves from nonprofessionals both in terms of the actual work each group performed and in status. Here, it is important to note that the status scores relate to education and income, and that the status distinction was accomplished in large part by a decline in the status of library assistants and not only by elevation in the status of librarians. As the status of librarians increased relative to other occupations after 1950, the status of library assistants steadily declined, until by 2000 it had fallen by half. In 1950, both librarians and library assistants were in the middle of the occupational status ranks. By 2000, librarians had edged into the upper 20 percent while assistants had fallen almost to the lowest 20 percent.

Librarians have not been particularly successful in advancing their status compared to that of the professionals with whom they would like to be peers. Librarians' view of desired peers at the outset of the MLS project differs from the classification of occupations by the U.S. Census Bureau, which has classified occupations at each census. The census classification of occupations has changed over time, becoming more detailed and more specific and recognizing new occupations as they have appeared. The title "librarian" has been used constantly from 1950 to 2000, but the occupations with which it has been grouped have varied. In 1950, 1960, and 1970, librarians were classified among "professional, technical, and kindred workers." In 1980 and 1990, librarians were classified with "professional specialty occupations." In 2000, librarians were classified with "education, training, and library occupations." By 2000, librarianship had come to be considered an education profession by the census.

From 1950 to 1990, librarianship ranked low compared to the status of other occupations within the same occupational category. The percentile rank of librarians among occupations in the same category ranged from 10 in 1950 to 17 in 1990. Table 3.3 shows the rank of librarianship among the professions included in its category for each census from 1960 to 1990.

Table 3.3. Rank of Librarians among Related Professions, by Occupational Status Score

Census	Number of occupations in census category with "librarians"	Percentile rank of librarians among occupations in same category
1950	49	10
1960	49	20
1970	126	19
1980	116	16
1990	106	17

Sources: See table 3.2.

The titles in the census classification of occupations change from census to census (the title librarian remains constant), so the rank of librarians is given as a percentile reflecting the percentage of other occupations in the category which rank lower. For example, a rank of 10 for 1950 indicates that librarianship had a higher occupational status score than 10 percent of the other occupations in its category. The data show that librarianship always ranked low among the occupations in its occupational category.

The 2000 census classified librarians among "education, training, and library occupations." There are fewer occupations (10) in this category than in the categories to which librarianship was previously assigned. In this category, librarianship ranks behind "other education, training, and library workers," postsecondary teachers, and elementary and middle school teachers. As shown in table 3.4, librarianship's status score is close

Table 3.4. Status of Education, Training, and Library Occupations 2000 Census

Occupation	Occupational Status Score	Rank in Census Category
Postsecondary teachers	86	2
Preschool and kindergarten teachers	45	7
Elementary and middle school teachers	83	3
Special education teachers	80	5
Other teachers and instructors	45	7
Archivists, curators, museum technicians	77	6
Librarians	82	4
Library technicians	22	9
Teacher assistants	32	8
Other education, training, and library workers	88	1

Source: Charles B. Nam and Monica Boyd, "Occupational Status in 2000: Over a Century of Census-Based Measurement," *Population Research and Policy Review* 23 (2004): 327–58.

to teachers' scores, while "library technicians" are far behind, at the bottom of the category.

PRESTIGE

Prestige studies differ from status studies in that they incorporate survey data about social prestige with census data to construct indexes of relative occupational prestige. Three major surveys have provided information used in prestige scoring of occupations: the National Opinion Research Council (NORC) survey of 1947, a set of NORC surveys conducted in 1963–1965, and the NORC General Social Survey of 1989.[12] Hauser and Warren recount the history of these occupational prestige studies.[13] Sociologists have offered variant procedures for combining survey prestige data with census occupational data, so direct comparison of scores across the body of studies is risky. The usefulness of these studies here is that they provide information about librarianship in relation to other occupations at decennial intervals. The outcomes of the various studies of prestige do correlate closely with one another, which suggests that relative prestige rankings are stable over time.[14] As Hauser and Warren argue, "However defined, there is substantial agreement about the properties of occupational prestige."[15]

For librarianship as an occupation, the body of prestige studies discloses a pattern similar to the pattern revealed by Nam's occupational status studies. Librarians have not made gains in prestige relative to the professionals to whom they compare themselves. Data from each census show librarianship has the lowest prestige among the traditional occupations to which it compares itself, except that librarians scored higher than programmers and systems analysts in 1970, the first year of reports for those two new occupations, and in 1990 for the first time librarians had higher prestige than clergy. The distance in prestige scores between librarians and library assistants was larger in 1990 than in 1950, so the MLS project succeeded in establishing librarians as superior to library technicians. Table 3.5 displays the prestige scores for librarianship and selected other professions as prestige was assessed by sociologists over the second half of the twentieth century.

As with the Nam-Powers occupational status scores, the prestige scores of librarianship were stable throughout the latter half of the twentieth century. The prestige data show (1) an increasing difference over time between the prestige scores of librarians and of library assistants and clerks, as the scores of the assistants declined, and (2) an increasing gap between the scores of librarians and those of the new computer-related occupations as the prestige of programmers and systems analysts increased.

Table 3.5. Occupational Prestige Scores 1950 to 1990

Occupation	1950	1960	1970	1980	1990
Librarian	60	55	55	54	50
Physician	92	82	81	86	81
Lawyer	93	76	75	75	80
Clergy	52	69	69	69	48
Engineer	84	74	63	65	65
College teacher	84	78	78	74	67
Elementary school teacher, public	72	60	59	64	60
Secondary school teacher, public	72	63	60	66	64
Computer programmer			51	61	59
Computer systems analyst			51	74	64
Library assistant/clerk	44	41	40	29	31

Sources: for 1950, Otis Dudley Duncan, "A Socioeconomic Index for All Occupations," in *Occupations and Social Status*, ed. Albert J. Reiss (New York: Free Press, 1961); for 1960, Paul Matthew Siegel, *Prestige in the American Occupational Structure*, doctoral dissertation, University of Chicago, 1971; for 1970, Inter University Consortium for Political and Social Research, "1970 Occupational Classification," http://webapp.icpsr.umich.edu/GSS/rnd1998/appendix/occu1970.htm; for 1980, Inter University Consortium for Political Research, "1980 Occupational Classification," http://webapp/icpsr.umich.edu/GSS/rnd1998/appendix/oc; for 1990, Robert M. Hauser and John Robert Warren, "Socioeconomic Indexes for Occupations: A Review, Update, and Critique," *Sociological Methodology* 27, no. 1 (1997): 177–298.

STATUS, PRESTIGE, STEREOTYPES, AND THE IMAGE OF THE LIBRARIAN

In 1876, when Melvil Dewey asserted that librarianship is a profession, he was calling for a new confidence among librarians and a new conception of librarians' work. Dewey grounded his view of librarians' importance in their role in selecting and organizing books and their influence on reading habits. He saw great power in the active role of shaping thought, a power not implied by the view of librarians as mere caretakers of books. Dewey declared that the old image of librarians and their work was inaccurate and that it was time for a new understanding of the personality of librarians, the kind of work they performed, and their place among the learned professions.[16] Dewey's concern about the image of librarians persists into the present.[17] The advocates of the MLS project in the 1940s did not allude to the image problem directly in discussions of accreditation, focusing instead on opportunities to increase professionalism and status. But they could not have been unaware of the image issue, as it was often discussed in librarians' professional literature and in conversations.

Studies of image and stereotype are important for creating a context for interpreting status and prestige scores such as the Nam-Powers score and the Socioeconomic Index (SEI). The Nam-Powers status scores are based on education and income, so with the increase in educational attainments of librarians, their status as measured by these scores rose. Whether their status increased as actually perceived subjectively by others in society is difficult to know without information about others' understanding of librarians' education and income. Librarians' incomes place them in the middle class, and income has a modest impact on their status relative to other occupations. It is librarians' education, having earned master's degrees, that gives them higher status scores. But if the public generally does not know that librarians have earned graduate degrees, then the Nam-Powers scores probably artificially inflate their actual status as perceived by the public at large.

Similarly, the SEI scores impute to librarians the prestige rankings of other occupations that are the direct object of survey studies. The assumption of the SEI is that insofar as librarianship is like occupations about which information is collected directly, it shares the same prestige. The validity of the SEI prestige score depends on the perceivers' actual knowledge of the characteristics of librarians.

There is visible evidence of income insofar as people conspicuously consume. Individuals and groups can make their income known to others through their conspicuous consumption behaviors. People believe they can guess others' income by looking at the ways they dress, where they live, the cars they drive, and the kinds of amusements with which they entertain themselves. People who vacation at ski resorts in Europe are believed to have more money than people who go cross-country skiing in the local state park. But education is not visible. People generally do not know that librarians are expected to earn accredited master's degrees, so the weight of education in calculating status and prestige scores may actually result in overestimates of librarians' standing.

INCOME

Librarians' incomes in the late 1940s were low compared to the incomes of people in other occupations. Librarians' earnings were comparable to those of public school teachers, but substantially less than the earnings of the more recognized professions, and in librarians' views, not commensurate with their levels of education and the importance of their work. In research for the Public Library Inquiry, Leigh found that the average librarian in 1949 earned $2,700 per year, less than the average factory worker, who earned $3,000.[18] The average earnings for an adult male who had attended college for four years or more was $6,179, substantially more than librarians earned.[19] When 1949 dollars are converted to 2007 dollars, the average professional librarian earned $26,515, only slightly more than the mean for all full-time employees ($24,724); the average library assistant earned $17,169. Table 3.6 shows librarians' earnings in 1949 compared to librarians' earnings in 2007. The table also includes income data for some of the occupations to which librarianship has compared itself and shows librarians' earnings as a percentage of these other occupations' earnings. The U.S. Department of Labor's National Compensation Survey reports mean and median annual earnings and weekly hours; means are reported here.[20]

One of the striking features of a comparison of earnings in 1949 and in 2007 is that almost all professional occupational groups had substantial real percentage increases in income. The latter half of the twentieth century was a time in which education made a big difference in earnings. Advocates of the MLS project were candid in stating their hopes that a new professional credential would lead to increased income for librarians, and they were right. Librarians believed their incomes should reflect their importance and their investments in their own education. Furthermore, they believed there should be a greater difference between the salaries of professional librarians and the salaries of library assistants. Professional librarians did indeed make salary gains between 1949 and 2007 at a rate much higher than the rate of all employed persons, and they did achieve a level of earnings substantially higher than library workers who do not

Table 3.6. Occupational Earnings 1949 and 2007

Occupation	Mean 1949 earnings in 2007 dollars	Mean 2007 earnings	% change 1949–2007	Professional librarian as % of other occupations 1949	Professional librarian as % of other occupations 2007
All full-time employees	$24,724	$42,504	72%	107%	126%
Professional librarians	$26,515	$53,518	102%	100%	100%
Library assistants/ technicians	$17,169	$30,521	78%	154%	175%
Physicians	$83,119	$167,767	102%	32%	32%
Lawyers	$69,297	$117,143	169%	38%	46%
College teachers	$36,809	$76,110	107%	72%	70%
Public school teachers	$26,185	$48,105	84%	101%	111%

Sources: Measuring Worth, www.measuringworth.com/uscompare/; U.S. Department of Labor, Bureau of Labor Statistics, "National Compensation Survey: Occupational Earnings in the United States, 2007," Bulletin 2704, August 2008, www.bls.gov; "Teachers' Pay Sets Mark," *New York Times*, March 1, 1952, 16; Lily Mary David, "Status of Library Employees," *ALA Bulletin*, November 1949, 331–3; U.S. Department of Commerce, Bureau of the Census, *Historical Statistics of the United States: Colonial Times to 1970* (Washington, D.C.: Government Printing Office, 1975).

have MLS degrees. Librarians' incomes increased 102 percent in 2007 dollars, while the mean increase for all full-time employees was only 72 percent. The salary gap within libraries, between professional librarians and library assistants/technicians, increased substantially. Rates of increase can be deceptive because when the base is low, a small absolute increase can produce a high percentage increase.

Librarians' salary increases after 1950 should be seen in context. The median income for persons over twenty-four years of age who held bachelor's degrees was $50,900 in 2006, while the median for those with master's degrees was $61,300 and the median for persons holding professional degrees was $100,000. Librarians with master's degrees had incomes well below the median for persons with comparable education.[21] In 2007, although librarians' earnings were closer to the earnings of lawyers than they had been in 1949 and they had moved further ahead of schoolteachers, they were still far below the premier professions.

Leigh compared librarians' earnings to factory workers' earnings in 1949. A pertinent question in the context of what differences the MLS project made concerning earnings is, who are the present income peers of librarians? John E. Buckley reported a list of all occupations ranked by salaries, based on 2000 census data.[22] Those data show that librarianship ranked 95 among 427 occupations, placing it below the top 20 percent of occupations. Library clerks ranked 344, slightly below animal caretakers and dress makers but above data entry keyers. Secondary school teachers ranked 56, elementary teachers 59, and actors and directors 68. Ranked close to librarians were funeral directors, urban planners, financial officers, supervisors, carpenters and related workers, public administrators, supervisors in extractive occupations, public relations specialists, and tile setters. Buckley presented salaries of postsecondary teachers by subject taught rather than collectively as "postsecondary teachers," and all teaching fields ranked above librarians. The earnings of librarians are comparable to the earnings of skilled craftspeople and those of professionals whose work does not require master's degrees.

NOTES

1. Samuel Haber, *The Quest for Authority and Honor in the American Professions, 1750–1900* (Chicago: University of Chicago Press, 1991).

2. Pierce Butler, "Librarianship as a Profession," *Library Quarterly* 21, no. 4 (1951): 235–47, 237.

3. American Association of School Librarians, "Position Statement on Instructional Classification, 2006," www.ala.org; Elizabeth A. Kaye, *Requirements for Cer-*

tification of Teachers, Counselors, Librarians, Administrators for Elementary and Secondary Schools, 73rd ed., 2008–2009 (Chicago: University of Chicago Press, 2008).

4. Association of College and Research Libraries, "Joint Statement on Faculty Status of College and University Librarians, 2007," www.acrl.org.

5. American Library Association, *Report on the State of Libraries, 2007*, www .ala.org.

6. Harris Poll 58, July 26, 2006, www.harrisinteractive.com.

7. "Jobs and Occupations: A Popular Evaluation," *Opinion News*, September 1, 1947, 3–13.

8. Michael I. Reed, "Expert Power and Control in Late Modernity: An Empirical Review and Theoretical Synthesis," *Organization Studies* 17, no. 4 (1996): 573–97.

9. Charles B. Nam and Monica Boyd, "Occupational Status in 2000: Over a Century of Census-based Measurement," *Population Research and Policy Review* 23 (2004): 327–58, 332.

10. Charles B. Nam and Mary G. Powers, *The Socioeconomic Approach to Status Measurement, with a Guide to Occupational and Socioeconomic Status Scores* (Houston, Tex.: Cap and Gown, 1983).

11. Nam and Boyd, "Occupational Status in 2000," 332.

12. National Opinion Research Center, "Occupational Prestige Studies/Summary," 2007, http://cloud9.norc.uchicago.edu/faqs/prestige.htm.

13. Robert M. Hauser and John Robert Warren, "Socioeconomic Indexes for Occupations: A Review, Update, and Critique," *Sociological Methodology* 27, no. 1 (1997): 177–298.

14. Keiko Nakao and Judith Treas, "The 1989 Socioeconomic Index of Occupations: Construction from the 1989 Occupational Prestige Scores," *GSS Methodological Report* 74 (Chicago: NORC, 1992); Hauser and Warren, "Socioeconomic Indexes for Occupations."

15. Hauser and Warren, "Socioeconomic Indexes for Occupations," 11.

16. Melvil Dewey, "The Profession," *American Library Journal* 1 (1876): 5–6.

17. Gary Mason Church, "In the Eye of the Beholder: How Librarians Have Been Viewed over Time," *Reference Librarian* 37, no. 78 (2002): 5–24.

18. Robert D. Leigh, *The Public Library in the United States: The General Report of the Public Library Inquiry* (New York: Columbia University Press, 1950).

19. Herman P. Miller, "Annual and Lifetime Income in Relation to Education: 1939–1959," *American Economic Review* 50, no. 5 (1960): 962–86, 966.

20. U.S. Department of Labor, Bureau of Labor Statistics, "National Compensation Survey: Occupational Earnings in the United States, 2007," www.bls.gov. Income data are collected and reported in a variety of ways. For librarians, some sources, such as the U.S. Census Bureau and the Bureau of Labor Statistics, report salaries for "librarians" and for "library assistants/clerks," and in 2007 "library technicians." The American Library Association salary reports are based on surveys of academic and public librarians, leaving out school, special, medical, and other kinds of librarians; the survey response rate is 31 percent. See American Library Association, *ALA-APA Salary Survey: A Survey of Public and Academic Library Positions Requiring an ALA-Accredited Master's Degree* (Chicago: ALA, 2006); *ALA-APA Salary Survey: A Survey of Public and Academic Library Positions Not Requiring an ALA-Accredited Master's Degree* (Chicago: ALA., 2006).

21. Sandy Baum and Jennifer Ma, *Education Pays 2007: The Benefits of Higher Education for Individuals and Society*, Trends in Higher Education Series, College Board, 2007, www.collegeboard.com.

22. John E. Buckley, "Rankings of Full-time Occupations, by Earnings, 2000," *Monthly Labor Review*, March 2002, 46–57.

4

✛

Recruitment
of New Librarians

Advocates believed that the MLS project would lead to more successful recruitment to the profession in terms of numbers and qualities
of applicants to programs. After a period of extensive unemployment of
librarians during the Depression, World War II brought a shortage of librarians as men were called into military service and women and men not
in the military found rewarding employment in industry.[1] In the postwar
period, librarians were concerned about a shortage of librarians, just as
other professional groups worried about filling their ranks in an uncertain
labor market. The shortage and its relation to library education was a continuing theme in the reports of the Board of Education for Librarianship.[2]
Changes in the system of library education were seen as an answer to
the problem. In her annual report to the profession on library education,
Anita Hostetter wrote in 1946, "The prevailing shortage of librarians appeared to some librarians as a handicap to progress which promised to
become permanent unless drastic changes in the present plan of library
education were put into immediate effect."[3] Library educators and leading librarians wanted to recruit more students into library schools, but
they also wanted to recruit students who had what they perceived to be
the correct qualities. The 1951 Standards for Accreditation, the founding
document of the MLS project, said, "Intellectual strength, personal bal-
ance and adjustment, aptitude for library service, and promise of professional purpose and development should be given primary consideration
in admitting students."[4]

37

THE SUPPLY OF LIBRARIANS

Library leaders thought that the fifth-year bachelor's degree was a barrier to recruitment into the profession because students did not believe that an investment of five years to earn a bachelor's degree was reasonable. A fifth-year bachelor's degree instead of a one-year master's degree, wrote academic librarian Lucy Fay, "starts the young librarian out with a feeling of frustration and with an inferiority complex in comparison with his friends and acquaintances working in other types of educational institutions."[5] Library educators and others believed that awarding a master's degree for that fifth year of study would make librarianship more attractive to students. However, both the enrollment in accredited programs and the number of graduates of accredited programs were stable from 1949 to 1959 (see table 4.1). The big boom in enrollments did not begin until 1959 and it lasted only until 1974. The number of graduates began to increase sharply in 1959 (most programs were one-year programs then) and grew until 1974. The numbers of graduates as reported in library school reports differ from the numbers of graduates reported by the National Center for Educational Statistics (NCES) in 1971 and 1976; the numbers for other report years are more consistent. The NCES reports include both ALA-accredited and nonaccredited programs.

By 1950, twenty-two accredited library programs were offering master's degrees.[6] It is unlikely that the shift from a bachelor's credential to a master's credential in itself caused an increase in enrollment; the increase in enrollment more closely followed market demand beginning in 1959 than it did the introduction of graduate programs. Increased enrollment in library schools was more likely a result of new opportunities for employment created by a combination of factors: the enrollment of Baby Boom children in schools, new federal aid for public libraries that financed new positions, and federal funding to support higher education through grants and loan programs that made it possible for more people to go to library school. Certainly postwar librarians were correct in predicting that there would be many new positions for librarians. The passage of the Baby Boom generation through the educational institutions that libraries serve was a major source of demand for new librarians, because the Baby Boom children were library users, whether in school, public, or academic libraries. New federal programs to assist libraries, beginning with the Library Services Act in 1957, provided public libraries, through the states, with funds to expand staff, creating new positions that called for new graduates. Federal aid to library education programs in the form of grants and loans to support graduate students began in the 1960s. In the first four years of the Title II-B program, 1,843 students received fellowships to earn master's degrees.[7]

Table 4.1. Enrollments and Graduates of Accredited Programs

Year	Enrollment in accredited programs	MLS graduates	Bachelors and MLS combined	Number of accredited schools
1949	2501	1612	1612	36
1950	2578	1355	1355	36
1951	2310	1289	1289	39
1952	2528	1580	1580	39
1953	2552	1581	1581	38
1954	2523	1698	1698	38
1955	2532	1351	1698	38
1956	2289	1264	1856	39
1957	2434	1399	1510	36
1958	2872	1263	1731	35
1959	3191	1544		33
1960	3263	1710		34
1961	3703	1715		36
1962	4175	1925		37
1963	4899	2188		36
1964	5782	2568		37
1965		2891		41
1966	6595	3338		44
1967	7974	3746		49
1968		4355		52
1969	8542	4513		55
1970	8933	5150		58
1971	10275	5451		58
1972	10521	5794		62
1973	10793	6059		65
1974		6323		69
1975		6319		69
1976		6045		69
1977		5498		69
1978		4724		71
1979	9180	4804		70
1980	8770	4670		71
1981	8868	3795		71
1982	7811			70
1983	8139	3784		70
1984	8548	3674		70
1985	8557	3231		69
1986	8921	3596		67
1987	10049	4058		64
1988	9864	3868		63
1989	9469	3793		63
1990	11020	4393		62
1991	12052	4699		60
1992	12379	5128		60

(continued)

Table 4.1.   (continued)

Year	Enrollment in accredited programs	MLS graduates	Bachelors and MLS combined	Number of accredited schools
1993	12069	4995		58
1994	11214	4805		58
1995	11746	4991		56
1996	12649	5271		56
1997	12480	5068		56
1998	12801	5024		56
1999	11241	5046		56
2000	13127	4877		56
2001	14043	4953		56
2002	15117	4923		56
2003	16876	5175		57
2004	17784	5951		57
2005	18271	6502		57
2006	17850			57
2007	18932			57
2008	19340			57

Sources: C. Edward Carroll, *The Professionalization of Education for Librarianship with Special Reference to the Years 1940–1960* (Metuchen, N.J.: Scarecrow, 1970), 61; "Enrollment Statistics for 32 Accredited Library Schools," *Journal of Education for Librarianship* 1, no. 1 (1960): 38–46; "Accredited Library School Enrollment Statistics: 1959–60," *Journal of Education for Librarianship* 4, no. 3 (1964): 169–81; "Accredited Library School Enrollment Statistics: 1962–63," *Journal of Education for Librarianship* 5, no. 2 (1964): 114–23; "Accredited Library School Enrollment Statistics: 1963–64," *Journal of Education for Librarianship* 7, no. 1 (1966): 29–41; William Landrom Williamson, "A Century of Students," *Library Trends* 34, no. 3 (1986): 433–49; *Library Human Resources: A Study of Supply and Demand*, report prepared for the National Center for Education Statistics and the Office of Libraries and Learning Technologies by King Research (Chicago: American Library Association, 1983), 31; American Library Association, Committee on Accreditation, "Statistical Data from Annual Review Reports, 1971–72 (Chicago: American Library Association, 1972); Association of American Library Schools, *Library Education Statistical Report* (State College, Pa.: Association of American Library Schools, 1980–82; Association for Library and Information Science Education, *Library and Information Science Education Statistical Report* (State College, Pa.: Association for Library and Information Science Education, 1983–2006); American Library Association, Committee on Accreditation, "Summary of Changes in ALA Accredited Programs," 2006–2009, www.ala .org. Data were not located for all years.

The enrollment in library schools and the supply of newly graduated librarians was steady from 1946 to 1959, but that level of production of graduates lagged behind the number of jobs available for new librarians in the 1950s, creating a shortage of librarians. Opportunities for employment and the shortage of librarians led to increased enrollment. The number of graduates increased sharply in the 1960s and 1970s, reaching a peak in 1974 that was not matched until 2005. In the late 1970s and through the 1980s, the number of graduates declined as sharply as it had risen in the 1960s. The boom in employment was followed by a bust in employment, and that led to an enrollment bust. The first indicators of decreases in job openings and salaries for new librarians appeared in the mid-1960s, and by the mid-1970s new librarians faced serious difficulties in finding employment in their chosen profession.[8] The situation was an excellent example of what Richard Freeman called "cobweb dynamics in the job market"—a shortage of graduates led to many employment opportunities, so many people were attracted to the field, resulting in large graduating classes and weak employment opportunities. The collapse in job opportunities occurred ahead of a decline in the production of graduates, which peaked in 1974, creating a period of oversupply. As Freeman says, "the supply of graduates is determined by market conditions several periods earlier, due to the fixed time delay in educational production, and is thus a lagging function of the state of the market."[9] The employment problems for new librarians coincided with a broad collapse in the American economy in the early 1970s.

The data on numbers of graduates are problematic. Uniform collected reports from library schools were not available until the Association of American Library Schools (AALS), which became the Association for Library and Information Science Education (ALISE), initiated a collaborative reporting process among the library schools in 1980. The ALA issued reports for accredited master's degrees for various years. However, not all reporters consistently differentiated between graduates of fifth-year BS programs and MLS programs, nor between accredited and nonaccredited master's programs. Numbers reported by Williamson in his history of library education, which Williamson says were based on *Library Journal* annual salary surveys, do not always match the numbers published in *Library Journal*.[10] The King Research study of library labor supply in 1980 reports numbers of graduates from a variety of sources, and those numbers are used in table 4.1 along with data from AALS and ALISE reports.[11] Not all schools report every year, so the numbers are not complete.

Although the accuracy of counts of graduates per year is questionable, the pattern of production of new librarians is clear. Enrollments grew rapidly from 1959 to the mid-1970s, then sharply declined when the supply of MLS graduates exceeded the demand for their services. Enrollment began to increase again in the late 1980s and grew strongly in the 1990s and early 2000s, although the number of graduates remained fairly steady from 1991 onward. The stability in the number of graduates (see table 4.1) in a period of strong enrollment increases is puzzling. The increasing disparity between the number of students enrolled and the number of graduates suggests either that many students are not completing degree programs or that students are taking progressively much longer to finish their degrees, even though the average length of degree programs has not increased, according to ALISE reports for 1991 and 2006.[12] If everyone who enrolled eventually graduated, and if students went through their programs at a steady pace, the number of enrollments and the number of

graduates would grow at similar rates, but the total enrolled is growing
much faster than the number of graduates. The ratio of master's degree
graduates to enrollments is shown in table 4.2.

Since 1950, the number of librarians has grown, but so have the sizes
of the whole labor force and the whole population. Comparison of the
growth in the number of persons employed as librarians to the growth of
all occupations shows that indeed the number of librarians as a percentage of the labor force almost doubled from 1950 to 2000, from 9 in 10,000
workers to 17 in 10,000. Most of the increase occurred from 1950 to 1970.

Table 4.2.   Ratio of Master's Graduates to Enrollments

Year	Graduations/ Enrollments	Year	Graduations/ Enrollments
1948	40%	1979	52%
1949	64%	1980	53%
1950	53%	1981	43%
1951	56%	1982	
1952	63%	1983	
1953	2%	1984	43%
1954	67%	1985	38%
1955	53%	1986	40%
1956	55%	1987	40%
1957	57%	1988	39%
1958	44%	1989	40%
1959	48%	1990	40%
1960	52%	1991	39%
1961	46%	1992	41%
1962	46%	1993	41%
1963	45%	1994	43%
1964	44%	1995	42%
1965		1996	42%
1966	51%	1997	41%
1967	47%	1998	39%
1968		1999	45%
1969	53%	2000	37%
1970	58%	2001	35%
1971	53%	2002	33%
1972	55%	2003	31%
1973	56%	2004	33%
1974		2005	36%
1975			
1976			
1977			
1978			

Source: See table 4.1.

Since 1970, the percentage of librarians in the workforce has been stable. Librarians still comprise a very small portion of the labor force, but they are a bigger small portion than they were sixty years ago. The portion of library technicians in the labor force changed from 3 in 10,000 to 11 in 10,000. Table 4.3 reports the number of librarians and other professionals and their percentages of the workforce from 1950 to 2000. Table 4.3 presents data about librarianship in the context of the professions to which librarians compare themselves. Except for the clergy, the leading professions and the educational professions grew as a segment of the labor force. Teachers at the K–12 levels grew strongly as a portion of the labor force until 1980 and have since been declining in numbers relative to other occupations.

Librarianship, like teaching, grew in the education years of the Baby Boom generation. The period of growth for librarianship ended in the 1970s. Since 1980, librarianship has been stable as a percentage of the workforce. The data in table 4.3 show that library assistants grew in numbers much faster than did librarians from 1950 to 1970, but they have since been in decline as a percentage of the workforce. The increase in the percentage of the labor force comprised by library assistants and technicians was more dramatic than the growth in the percentage of librarians, increasing nearly sixfold in the same time that the percentage of librarians nearly doubled (1950–1970). These differences suggest that in the early years of the MLS project, positions for library assistants grew rapidly because this was the period in which there was a shortage of librarians, so the need was met by library assistants. After 1970, however, there was no shortage of librarians. Their rate of employment has remained constant

Table 4.3. Professions as Percentage of the Workforce

Occupation	% of Workforce					
	1950	*1960*	*1970*	*1980*	*1991*	*2000*
Librarian	0.09	0.12	0.17	0.19	0.17	0.17
Physician	0.35	0.38	0.39	0.44	0.49	0.53
Lawyer	0.31	0.33	0.36	0.51	0.64	0.65
Clergy	0.30	0.32	0.31	0.29	0.28	0.27
College teacher	0.24	0.30	0.68	0.64	0.66	0.71
Elementary teacher, public school	1.19	1.60	1.98	2.34	1.30	0.16
Secondary teacher, public school	0.70	0.92	1.38	0.87	1.05	0.98
Computer programmer	0.00	0.01	0.22	0.32	0.47	0.52
Computer systems analyst	0.00	0.01	0.14	0.21	0.58	1.33
Library assistant/technician	0.03	0.06	0.17	0.14	0.13	0.11

Sources: Robert F. Szafran, "Measuring Occupational Change over Four Decennial Censuses, 1950–1980," *Work and Occupations* 19, no. 3 (1992): 293–326; *Statistical Abstract of the U.S.*, 1992, 2001.

while library assistants' percentage of the labor force has declined. In addition to the end of the shortage of librarians, technological change in the decades since 1970 enabled implementation of automation to carry out many routine library functions, and much of library assistants' work has been transferred to computers.

The data in table 4.3 reveal a stronger resemblance between librarianship and education as occupations than between librarianship and computer-related professions. Computer programmers and computer systems analysts together have grown dramatically and consistently and now form nearly 2 percent of the workforce. Computers and software have become the principal tools of librarians, but librarians are consumers of the work of the computer-based professions, not the creators of computers and systems.

Whether the growth in the number of positions for new librarians in the 1950s and 1960s was due to a major change in American society's demand for additional library services or whether it was due simply to population growth is debatable. The adequacy of the supply of librarians is usually discussed in the profession's literature in terms of unfilled positions in libraries. Another way to look at the supply is in terms of the ratio of librarians to the potential service population. The service population for school librarians as a whole is the number of K–12 students and teachers; for academic libraries, it is the number of faculty plus the number of persons enrolled in colleges and universities; and for public libraries, it is the whole population. Defining the service population for special libraries would be a formidable task. Data on the number of new librarians who prepared for each type of library service are not available, but data on changes in the whole population size are. If the definition of a librarian is one who graduates from an accredited program, it is possible at least to determine the maximum possible number of new librarians each year because it is the same as the number of graduates. From 1940 to 1949, the accredited library education programs awarded 12,650 bachelor's or master's degrees. The increase in population from the 1940 to the 1950 census was 20.149 million, so the increase in population was 1,594 persons per new librarian. Things got worse in the 1950s. These numbers show why librarians at the time felt there was a shortage—the increase in numbers of professional librarians was not keeping pace with the increase in population. And since 1940 it has not, although recently things have not been worsening as fast as they were in the 1940s and 1950s (see table 4.4).

There are some shaky assumptions involved in this approach to counting new librarians: that everyone who graduates goes to work in the profession, and continues to work at least through the decade; that persons are not earning degrees to keep jobs they already hold; and that there are not large numbers of immigrants, unless the immigrants are from Can-

Table 4.4.   Ratio of New Librarians to New Population

Decade	New librarians (graduates of accredited programs)	Difference in U.S. population from previous census (in thousands)	Increase in population per new librarian
1940–1949	12,640	20,149 (1950–1940)	1594
1950–1959	15,842	28,400 (1960–1950)	1793
1960–1969	28,949	24,381 (1970–1960)	842
1970–1979	56,167	22,674 (1980–1970)	404
1980–1989	34,469	22,406 (1990–1980)	650
1990–1999	49,420	32,302 (2000–1990)	654

Sources: See table 4.1; *Historical Statistics of the United States, Millennial Edition Online,* http://hsus .cambridge.org; U.S. Census Bureau, The 2009 Statistical Abstract, www.census.gov.

ada, because graduates from accredited programs in Canada are included in the totals. Despite these qualms, the number of graduates is at least an indicator of changes in the supply of librarians, and that indicator shows that after a slow start, the life span of the MLS project has been a period of improvement over the situation in the 1940s and 1950s.

The way that people report their occupations affects occupational data. Persons may report themselves as librarians who do not hold ALA-accredited MLS degrees. As Kutzik pointed out, many people may describe themselves as librarians who do not hold the MLS degree.[13] When alternative names are suggested for them, they may respond with some resentment, insisting that they are in fact librarians by virtue of the work they do, not by virtue of degrees they may or may not have earned.[14] The 1983 King Report for the ALA observed that the census count is based not on the credentials one holds but on the actual work one says one does, and "people tend to classify themselves in higher status jobs than would an objective interviewer."[15] So whether the numbers are problematic would seem to be a matter of where one stands on the question of whether an occupation is defined by a credential one holds, as in the King Report, or by the work that a person actually does.

The Public Library Inquiry found that less than half the librarians in the United States had the education called for by the American Library Association. Fifty years later, the U.S. Census found that 3,527 academic libraries employed 95,665 full-time-equivalent staff, 26 percent of whom were librarians. In 2003, 9,211 public libraries employed a full-time-equivalent staff of 136,172. The number of librarians employed in public libraries was 45,115, of whom 30,479 held master's degrees in library science. After fifty years of the MLS project, the portion of public librarians who held the credential called for by their job title had increased from 48 percent to 66 percent.[16] That is a substantial increase. Still, more than one-third of public librarians do not hold what the ALA considers the proper credential.

RECRUITMENT AND THE CHARACTERISTICS OF LIBRARIANS

The urgency of recruiting people into librarianship was one of the reasons for making a change in the structure of library education in the 1940s. Contemporary commentators on library education recognized that their hopes for a more respected occupation rested heavily on the kinds of persons who earned the MLS. The MLS was part of a strategy intended to attract the persons librarianship wanted: bright young people with strong liberal arts backgrounds. The 1951 Standards said students should be intelligent and well adjusted, should have an aptitude for library service, and should show potential for professional development. Ralph Beals of the Graduate Library School at the University of Chicago spoke for many when he argued that students should come to school with a good general education.[17]

A sketch of desired students is provided by Willard Mishoff's summary in 1952 of admissions policies for MLS programs: "Library schools generally require for entrance (a) graduation from an approved college or university; (b) a superior undergraduate record; (c) evidence, through credit or examination, of a mastery of fundamental library techniques; and (d) a reading knowledge of at least one foreign language. Skill in typewriting is usually expected of library school students." Reflecting the 1951 Standards, Mishoff noted that "library schools judge applicants especially as to their intellectual capacity, personality, aptitude for library service, and promise of professional growth."[18] Robert Hayes conducted a survey of library school deans in 1993 and concluded that admissions criteria "universally emphasize a 'liberal arts' program for the bachelor's degree" but as a desirable, not a necessary criterion. Hayes also found that "Every program makes a conscious effort to evaluate the student not only on the basis of academic performance but on the basis of personal qualities—motivation, personality, maturity, etc.," using such devices as personal essays, reference letters, and interviews; clear definitions of what the schools meant by personal qualities did not emerge from his study.[19] Data relating to personality variables have never been reported systematically by the library schools, so whether the MLS project succeeded in recruiting persons with the desired qualities must be inferred from a variety of sources. It is difficult to identify substantive data that support operational and comparable measures of such qualities as intellect, personality, aptitude, and promise.

Recruitment, image, and characteristics of librarians are interrelated topics. The kinds of persons who enter the profession play major roles in defining what the profession will be and how it will be perceived, just as its perception and image play a role in determining the kinds of persons who will find the profession attractive. Recruitment, image, and characteristics are reflexive and inseparable. A national opinion poll of 1,357 adults in 1950 revealed that not many saw librarianship as a good career choice for young women. The poll inquiring about "Careers Recommended for Young Girls" revealed that only 2 percent of respondents would have advised a woman to seek a career in librarianship (see table 4.5). The survey characterized all the occupations as professions; as early as 1950, the words "occupation" and "profession" had come to be used as synonyms; while librarianship was chasing the professional label, the discriminating power of the label itself had been weakened. Even in 1963, after the boom in librarianship had begun, a survey of high school students' views of occupational prestige ranked librarian as 61 among 117 occupations (behind file clerk) and library assistant as 76 (behind factory

Table 4.5. Careers Recommended for Young Girls in 1950

Poll question: Suppose a young girl came to you and asked your advice about taking up a profession. Assuming that she was qualified to enter any of these professions, which one of them would you first recommend (suggest) to her?

Career	% Yes
Actress	3
Airline stewardess	4
Beautician	2
Department store sales	1
Dietician	8
Doctor, dental technician	2
Dressmaker, fashions	4
Journalism	3
Librarian	2
Modeling	2
Musician	2
Nursing	28
Secretarial career	8
Social service worker	7
Teaching	16
Other	3
Don't know, no answer	5

Source: Gallup Poll, 1950, Public Opinion Online, Roper Center at University of Connecticut.

sewing machine operator).[20] The proponents of the MLS project believed that one of the outcomes of elevating the credentials of librarians would be a change in the public assessment of the prestige of librarianship, and thus would lead more talented young people to want to be librarians. Exactly how that would happen was not explained at the time. Librarians just believed that if they built more prestigious (meaning graduate) educational programs, more people, and more of the sort they wanted, would come to them.

The popular image of the librarian was much discussed among librarians. Research on image has often been related to study of personality type in order to determine whether personality tests support or contradict the stereotype of librarians. Two studies conducted about the time that the MLS project began provide bases for understanding how librarianship was seen at the time and how its perception has changed since. As part of the Public Library Inquiry, Alice Bryan and her colleagues surveyed more than 2,395 public librarians. The survey included a personality test, the results of which showed few differences between male and female librarians: "the typical female librarian has a personality profile that is remarkably similar to that of her male colleague." Bryan found that librarians were submissive in social situations, felt inferior and lacked self-confidence, but in general were "reasonably well adjusted."[21] In 1947–1948, Robert Douglass surveyed the general literature and the professional literature of librarianship to see what the stereotype of librarian was, then surveyed 525 library school students about the traits he had identified. He found that the impression held by library school students was consistent with the general public's and professional librarians' views: "Librarians are more introspective than other people, more deferential to authority, more orderly, and more conscientious. The 125 library school men also perceived them to be less self-confident and less innovative and creative than people in general."[22]

Douglass's was one of many studies from 1940 onward that came to similar conclusions and thus validated the stereotype. In a review of these studies through the 1970s, Agada concluded that librarians in general were shown by personality studies to be more submissive and deferential than normal, to be less confident, to feel inferior, and to be more isolated, less aggressive, and less dominant than the average person.[23] However, in a 1990 study of 380 Michigan librarians, David found that librarians, regardless of the type of library in which they were employed and regardless of their subspecialty, could be described as consistently "artistic" in the schema she used, meaning they perceived themselves to be "expressive, original, intuitive, nonconforming, introspective, independent, [and] disorderly," preferring "artistic occupations or situations" and valuing "esthetic qualities."[24] Grimes contends that studies such as David's show a shift in librarians' personality types that presents them as more oriented to the social aspect of their work but not comfortable with bureaucratic rules: "The pattern that emerges in the 1990s is of an updated female 'Marian' / male 'Marion' who has been, since the 1940s, consistently intelligent, introverted, self-sufficient and interested in a life of the mind and in the arts. At the same time, studies in recent years show more interest by librarians in social services and people-oriented work than in the past."[25]

Image continues to be a popular topic among librarians. Findings of studies concerning stereotypes and librarians' own insecurities about their image are convincing in part because they are so consistent.[26] In a survey of the literature on the media representations and the public image of librarians, Seale concluded that while the public sees librarians as helpful persons, they do not perceive librarians as professionals. "Overall," she writes, "the public is unfamiliar with education, knowledge, skills and duties of librarians."[27] What the public is familiar with is a set of media representations of librarians, which Seale summarizes as Old Maid, Policeman, Librarian as Parody, Inept Librarian, and Hero (Buffy the Vampire Slayer).

In 1982, Pauline Wilson reviewed and synthesized the research on the image of librarians and concluded that the image was consistent and that the practices in library education continued to be a key element of the problem. Wilson argued that librarianship was responsible for its own stereotype and for the sense of identity that librarians had collectively developed. The problem, she said, lies "with the stereotype and, most especially, with self-perception, with the self-image, the minority mind set librarians have developed as a result of the stereotype." Persons considering librarianship as a potential career, she said, were influenced by librarians' recruiting activities and by the attractiveness of the stereotype to some candidates. "It is librarians and the stereotype that do the major recruiting," she wrote.[28] In the 1980s, the ALA sponsored a series of committee meetings and workshops concerning recruitment and launched its "Each One Reach One" campaign, to assure that librarians continued to influence students.[29] Subsequent studies of factors impacting students' decisions to enter library school have consistently found that librarians had influential roles.[30] Library schools focus much of their recruiting activity in library publications and exhibits and presentations at library conferences. Librarianship, as Wilson said, has been self-perpetuating because it recruits those who are influenced successfully by librarians.

The image and stereotype of librarians has not changed much in fifty years, nor has the personality profile as indicated by a variety of studies.[31] The impacts that image and stereotype have on recruitment are unclear. We do not know, for example, how many people turn away from librarianship because they do not wish to be associated with librarians, or because they see librarianship as a low status field. A 1970 study that would bear replication showed that students in fields other than library school rated the status of librarianship sharply below the rating that library science students gave it.[32] Bambi Burgard suggests that females who do not fit librarians' psychological stereotype would not be interested in librarianship. She found that "women in academic majors leading to traditionally male-dominated career paths [which would not include librarianship] demonstrated significantly higher levels of competitiveness, masculinity, and masculinity-femininity and significantly lower levels of femininity than women in traditionally female-dominated academic majors."[33] Rebecca Watson-Boone surveyed graduates of eight liberal arts colleges from 1962 to 2000 who had entered librarianship and found that 57 percent said they held a positive image of librarians after college, a percentage that increased to 70 percent after completing a graduate library school program; 12 percent held a negative image of librarians after college and 6 percent a mixed image; then after library school, only 8 percent held a negative image but 15 percent had developed a mixed image.[34]

It is difficult to assess whether the image of librarians is accurate or whether it is a result of public ignorance about librarians, the manipulative power of popular culture media, or a failure of librarians to explain themselves through marketing. Whether problems of image and personality are due to a failing of library education and whether library educators ought to base admissions and graduation on personality assessments are debatable questions. To let personality assessment intrude into assessment of potential for academic performance would open a door to kinds of discrimination that are contrary to principles of education, and to a line of reasoning that could lead to institutionalizing sets of invidious distinctions based on criteria that fail tests of ethics and law. Library schools, like most other university programs, have been loath to use such criteria.

The MLS project has had no discernible impact on the image of librarians or on librarians' personality types as measured by a variety of researchers. The degree requirement may have been an irrelevant factor in the persistence of the image of librarians—the public generally does not know about the MLS. Or it may be that, as Wilson charged, the professions' recruiting practices and the library schools' admissions processes have abetted preservation of a particular type of person who plays the role of librarian. Studies that focus on the personality characteristics of one group without presenting them in larger social contexts may lead to unsound conclusions. A more contextual approach is exemplified by Williamson, Pemberton, and Lounsbury, whose 2005 study of personality traits and job satisfaction among information professionals revealed that the traits that characterize job and career satisfaction among these persons are the same traits that characterize satisfaction among other occupations: emotional resilience, work drive, and optimism.[35] More studies that compare librarians to other groups, rather than studies of librarians in isolation, might help librarianship to understand itself better. However librarianship understands or thinks of itself, clearly the MLS project did not lead to a change in the popular perception of librarians. The stereotype of the dour old maid continues to live in the public mind.

Data concerning the characteristics and demographic variables of librarians and library school students have been collected only sporadically. The American Library Association has not collected much data about the characteristics of librarians, nor have the library schools reported data about students. The Bureau of Education for Librarianship did not collect extensive data on the characteristics of library school students in the 1940s. The Public Library Inquiry collected some data on library school students. The profile that emerges there presents library school students as mostly part-time (58 percent), female (88 percent among undergraduates, 78 percent among graduate students), college graduates (61 percent) working toward their first professional degree, most of whom lived in the metropolitan area of their library schools. Leigh expanded on their characteristics based on admissions requirements. Library schools were not selective in their admissions in the sense that they limited enrollments or treated candidates as competitors for places, then and now. Leigh expected that under the new MLS programs, admissions criteria would limit acceptance to those who were in the upper half of their undergraduate class, but that a qualitative approach would be taken to grades as well as to Graduate Record Exam (GRE) scores to account for late bloomers and people with "unorthodox abilities." Generally, the schools did not require specific undergraduate majors but advocated general studies. Most required mastery of some language other than English. Leigh found no clear statements about the role of personality factors in admissions. He expressed confidence that the schools might "get more than their share of the decent, reliable, public-spirited, orderly minded, intellectually superior members of the year's [bachelor's degree] graduates."[36]

At about the same time, Douglass collected informative data about the characteristics of 525 men and women enrolled in accredited library education programs in 1947–1948.[37] Students from seventeen of the thirty-six schools voluntarily participated in his study. The characteristics of students that emerge from Douglass's research support and amplify the findings of the Public Library Inquiry. Data about his sample are valuable because they include so many students from about half the library schools just at the moment that the Board of Education for Librarianship suspended accreditation to enable a shift to the MLS. Douglass's work provides good information about the characteristics of those who sought to become librarians at the time the MLS project was starting. Douglass's data show the typical library school student to have been a single person, recently graduated from college, who sought a career in management or public services of some kind in an academic or public library, with some showing interest in school or special libraries. Although data on the academic standing of these students were not collected, otherwise these students appear to meet the criteria suggested in the goals of the MLS project and the 1951 ALA standards.

The profile of students enrolled in library school a generation after the MLS project began is quite different, however. Heim and Moen surveyed library school students in 1988 in a study prepared for the ALA Office of Library Personnel Resources.[38] They used different categories to collect data than Douglass did, but the findings of the study can be compared to show changes in library school students as the Baby Boom generation replaced its predecessor. Table 4.6 presents a comparison of findings from the studies. In the forty years between the surveys, library school students became older, were more likely to be married, had more years of formal education, experienced longer intervals between undergraduate study and entrance to library school, and were less interested in public and academic libraries. The collective portrait shows that clearly many boomer students came to librarianship as a second career or after some other postgraduate activity, such as raising a family. One-fourth already held a graduate degree in some other field. These data do not bear out the hopes of the MLS project. Instead of attracting liberally educated young people directly from arts and sciences undergraduate programs, library schools became populated by middle-aged, second-career students.

The percentage of students reporting an interest in school librarianship is small in both studies, which might seem odd, given that school librarians are the largest single group of librarians when considered by type of library. The reason that school library aspirants are not strongly represented in either sample is that school librarians very often do not enroll to seek master's degrees but instead enroll in certificate programs, many persons studying for school librarianship do so in schools that do not have ALA-accredited master's programs, and many school librarians, particularly in 1948 and 1988, are teachers who are appointed to the role, and thus use the title but have no library school education at all. While most schools with accredited programs closed their undergraduate majors by 1988, many undergraduate programs at other schools remained. In 1985–1986, 527 students were enrolled in 25 undergraduate programs; 49 percent of the graduates of these programs were placed in school libraries, 14 percent in public libraries, and the rest in academic, special, and "other" employment settings.[39] So, in addition to showing that the MLS project failed to attract the kinds of students sought, the data show

Table 4.6.   Traits of Library School Students

Students Characteristics	1947–48 %	1969 %	1988 %
Marital status			
single	78	38	42
married	17	42	52
divorced, widowed, separated	5	7	6
Highest degree held			
none	8		0
bachelor's	83		75
master's	8		22
doctoral	0.4		3
Interval between college graduation and library school enrollment			
less than 1 year	26	25	0
1–3 years	32		21
4–6 years	21		15
7–9 years	6		19
10 or more years	15		45
Work preference			
academic	38	25	23
public	34	22	19
special	16	15	36
school	8	30	10
government	4		13
other		7	
Type of work preference			
reference and bibliography	29	22	34
administration	18	13	6
children and youth	17		12
technical processes	10	12	16
circulation	7		
readers advisory	5		
general	3		
personnel	1		
public relations	2	4	
library school teaching	1		
other	6		6
computers, systems	1	12	
independent (broker, consultant)	6		
further graduate study		4	
special clientele		30	
special collections		7	
general public services	4		

Note: The surveys did not all ask the same questions, so there are no responses listed for questions asked in different years. White and Macklin did not collect data about marital status of men, 16 percent of the respondents to their study.

Sources: Robert R. Douglass, *The Personality of the Librarian*, doctoral dissertation, University of Chicago, 1957; Rodney F. White and David B. Macklin, *Education, Careers, and Professionalization in Librarianship and Information Science, Final Report* (Washington, D.C.: Office of Education, Bureau of Research, 1970); Kathleen M. Heim and William E. Moen, *Occupational Entry: Library and Information Science Students' Attitudes, Demographics, and Aspirations Survey* (Chicago: American Library Association, 1989).

that the project was unsuccessful in providing graduate library science credentials for school librarians.

It would be useful to have a current study of the characteristics of library school students to see whether the newer generation of library school students is different from the boomer generation, which now occupies most of the library positions but no longer dominates library school enrollment. In the past twenty years, research on student characteristics has focused on the variables by which schools and the profession interpret diversity. Data collected by ALISE in the annual reports do not present a complete picture of students. The ALA has only recently begun to collect data about its own members. These data may someday enable longitudinal studies of characteristics of the members of the profession. The discussion that follows is based on data that are available concerning the academic backgrounds and ages of the men and women who have come to library school under the MLS project.

ACADEMIC BACKGROUNDS

The MLS project was intended to enhance the quality of librarianship by attracting more talented people to the profession. In 1950, there was less contention than there is presently about concepts such as intelligence, ability, talent, academic potential, and even what constitutes academic success; in recent decades, these terms have been challenged in a variety of ways. Despite the arguments about such matters, library schools and other academic entities have had to make choices in admissions processes and have had to evaluate the work of their students. Data about academic prowess, however, is scarce. Individual schools may have collected such data, but general reports are rare. Researchers compiling data about the first four years of the Title II-B fellowship program for library school students complained in 1970 that although the schools required GRE scores and used them as selection tools, only half the deans could report them. Data on students may exist in accreditation reports, but these are closely held and idiosyncratically designed.

To evaluate potential for success in graduate study, many library schools have used the GRE. By 1966, 75 percent of library schools were using GRE scores as factors in selecting students for Title II-B fellowships, although it is not clear whether they were using the scores as admission criteria.[40] Fasik reported in 1986 that reliance on grade point average and GRE scores was replaced in the 1980s by other criteria such as reference letters, interviews, and essays. She reported that the new "flexibility" in admissions standards was due to sharp drops in the number of applicants and to increasing competition among schools as overall enrollment plunged in the 1980s.[41] In 1986, Wilson argued that library schools should not admit "marginal" students but did so because there were too many schools and thus they competed among themselves for the enrollments essential to their institutional survival.[42] Wilson advocated the stringent use of accreditation as a way to force library schools to admit and prepare better students, and thus eventually produce better graduates, who eventually would change the social stereotype.

The test scores of those interested in librarianship who took the GRE during the last fifty years provide an indicator of the relative academic qualifications of applicants. Table 4.7 shows mean scores for selected dates (scores for each year were not found). The mean scores of those who took the GRE between 2003 and 2007 with the declared intent to major in library science were in the 70th percentile on the test of verbal ability, in the 35th percentile on the test of quantitative ability, and in the 54th percentile on the test of analytical writing (GRE 2007). The number of the test takers who were actually admitted to library schools and their GRE scores are not known, but these test data reveal that the individuals who said they wanted to become librarians had above average verbal skills,

Table 4.7. GRE Scores of Potential Library Science Students (mean test scores of test takers who declared intent to study library science)

	1981–83	1983–86	1985–88	1992–95	2003–06
n with intent to enter library school	1882	2515	2543	3181	3002
Verbal Scores					
mean for all	na	475	478	479	465
mean for Lib Sci	534	536	534	524	537
Percentile of Lib Sci mean	na	59–65th	62–66th	63–68th	64–68th
Quantitative Scores					
mean for all	na	546	553	555	584
mean for Lib Sci	486	485	487	500	541
Percentile of Lib Sci mean	na	29–34th	51–56th	36–39th	23–36th
Analytical Scores					
mean for all	na	516	523	543	4.1
mean for Lib Sci	na	529	527	554	4.5
Percentile of Lib Sci mean		40–46th	47–52nd	46–50th	54th

Sources: Educational Testing Service, *Guide to the Use of the Graduate Record Examinations Program and Guide to the Use of Scores,* www.ets.org.

below average quantitative skills, and about average analytical skills compared to the population who took the tests. Whether those who took the tests were more talented in these regards than the general population of graduate student applicants is an interesting question. Whether graduate programs admitted the average test takers, in library science or in other fields, is another interesting question. Both questions could be avenues for research.

Average scores on GRE tests declined after 1967 just as SAT scores did.[43] Since the percentile for applicants to library schools stayed about the same, about the 60th percentile, it is reasonable to conclude that the scores of those interested in library school declined along with the average. The pool of students from whom library schools could draw did change during the period, as did their scores on standardized tests. The number of reports for persons interested in library science is so far below the enrollment numbers for library schools that one must conclude most library schools are not requiring GRE scores for entrance. The first year of GRE reports of these scores is 1976; the first library science scores located are 1981–1983. GRE reports indicate the percentile of scores by intervals but not the percentile for each exact score.

ALISE does not gather data about academic performance of students. Studies in 1970 and 1988 presented data concerning students' performance as measured by grades.[44] These studies showed students' grade point averages in graduate library school were much higher than their undergraduate grade point averages. Whether the increase is a result of more diligence in graduate school, more intellectual maturity, an easier curriculum, less competition, or grade inflation cannot be known until schools begin publishing more data about their students. Grade inflation became apparent at all levels and all kinds of schools after 1970 and continues.[45] In most graduate schools, grades below B do not earn credit toward graduation, so there is a tendency for faculty to grade on an A–B scale rather than an A–F scale, and to use grades of C rather than D or F to encourage students who are performing poorly to drop out, or to force them out.

THE AGE OF LIBRARIANS

In the 1940s, some library school faculties and even the Board of Education for Librarianship discouraged those younger than age thirty from seeking entry to the profession.[46] One of the goals of the MLS project was to make the profession more attractive to young people by offering a higher credential for five years of study. What happened, however, is that the age of library school students increased throughout the last half of the century. In 1948, 63 percent of library school students were under the age of thirty. By 1982, only 47 percent were, and the percentage of students under thirty steadily declined until bottoming at 30 percent in 1989. Since then, the percentage of library school students less than thirty has hovered around 35 percent. The age pattern of library school students established by the Baby Boom generation persists.

One reason for the increase in age of library school students might be that the master's requirement, like the fifth-year bachelor's degree, dissuaded young people from pursuing professional education for librarianship, having an effect opposite to the intended impact. Instead, library education became a vehicle for those seeking a second career, or for women who had raised families before seeking professional education. Another possibility is that experienced nonprofessionals working in libraries began to seek master's degrees in substantial numbers. Still another possibility is that as the requirements for school library certification became more rigorous, experienced teachers constituted a more substantial portion of enrollment. In 1960, 18 of 31 accredited programs had an upper age limit of thirty-five as an admission criterion, which suppressed enrollment of older persons who might have wanted to become librarians.[47] In the 1960s and 1970s, library schools began changing their requirements. Williamson observed that when the median age of library school students had risen above thirty in the 1980s, "library schools generally abandoned their policies of discouraging applicants above that age."[48] Whether the decision to admit older students reflected yielding to pressure from adults who wanted to enter library schools, or whether library schools needed students and were encouraging enrollments by eliminating the age barrier to admissions, is unclear; definitive statements would require a case-by-case investigation of library school policies and, more difficult, of the academic debates and reasoning underlying the policy shifts.

The Board of Education for Librarianship and the Committee on Accreditation did not gather data on characteristics of students other than numbers of enrollments, sex, and after 1970, ethnicity. When ALISE began publishing reports in 1981, it gathered information about ages of students from the schools. Table 4.8 presents data concerning students' ages for the years data were collected. The table also includes data from Douglass's study, collected in 1948, and from White's and Macklin's survey of students enrolled in library schools in 1969, which drew responses from 3,516 students. There was a major shift in the age distribution of students between 1948 and 1969, which was even more pronounced by 1982. There was a substantial increase in age by 1969, mostly among women (men were only 16 percent of student respondents). Between 1948 and 1969, enrollment of students under age twenty-five slipped from 63 percent to 39 percent, while enrollment of students over age forty grew from 8 percent

Chapter 4

**Table 4.8. Ages of Enrolled Library Education Students
(percentage in age groups, by year)**

age group	20–29	30–39	40–49	50+			
1948	63	29	7	1			

age group	<25	26–30	31–40	40+			
1969	39	19	21	20			

age group	20–24	25–34	35–44	45–54	55+		
1981	19	53	20	7	1		

age group	20–24	25–29	30–34	35–39	40–44	45–49	50+
1982	17	30	23	14	8	4	4
1983	16	30	23	14	9	5	4
1984	14	29	22	16	10	5	4
1985	13	27	22	18	11	6	4
1986	11	25	21	18	13	6	6
1987	10	23	20	19	16	7	6
1988	10	21	19	20	16	8	6
1989	9	21	19	19	16	10	6
1990	10	21	18	19	17	9	5
1991	11	21	17	17	17	10	6
1992	12	22	16	16	17	11	6
1993	12	23	16	15	16	11	7
1994	13	22	15	14	17	12	7
1995	13	24	16	14	14	12	7
1996	12	24	16	14	15	12	8
1997	12	26	16	12	14	12	8
1998	11	25	16	12	13	13	9
1999	12	25	17	12	13	12	9
2000	12	24	16	13	13	13	10
2001	11	22	19	13	12	12	11
2002	data not available						
2003	13	24	18	13	11	10	11
2004	12	25	18	13	11	10	12
2005	13	25	17	13	11	9	11

Note: 1948 is based on Douglass (1957) sample of 525.
Sources: Robert R. Douglass, *The Personality of the Librarian,* doctoral dissertation, University of Chicago,
1957; Rodney F. White and David B. Macklin, *Education, Careers, and Professionalization in Librarianship and Information Science, Final Report* (Washington, D.C.: Office of Education, Bureau of Research,
1970); Association of American Library Schools, *Library Education Statistical Report,* 1981, 1982; Association for Library and Information Science Education, *Library and Information Science Education Statistical
Report,* 1983–2006.

to 20 percent. This increase in older students was prior to the arrival of
the Baby Boom generation in graduate programs; once that generation
arrived, it sustained the pattern of enrollment of older students.

During the last two decades, about a third of library school students
were in their twenties, a third were in their thirties, and a third were forty

or older. In 1989, the percentage of students under age thirty reached its lowest level, 30 percent, and by 2005 it had risen to 38 percent. In the same period, the number of students over fifty had increased from 6 percent to 11 percent. These data are for all students, not graduates, so if data for graduates were available (ALISE does not collect data on the age of graduates), they would show the entrants to the profession were even older. The shift in age of students and graduates likely has had several consequences. As the age of students increased, so also did the gap in time between graduation from college and entry to library school. Older persons have to become reacculturated to the role of student. Librarians who start their careers in their forties or fifties, as fully a third do, have shorter careers; consequently, they have less time to achieve advanced positions. Older graduates also have less time to build on the knowledge acquired during schooling through experience and advanced professional development.

There is a widespread concern about the "graying" of the profession expressed in conference programs, editorials, and essays. In 2008, the ALA Office of Research and Statistics conducted a survey which asked library directors for estimates of staff ages. The survey found that 7 percent were estimated to be under thirty, 19 percent were age thirty to thirty-nine, 35 percent were age forty to forty-nine, 32 percent were age fifty to fifty-nine, and 7 percent were sixty or older.[49] One-third of students were over forty (see table 4.8), so many of the replacements coming along are also "gray."

UNDERGRADUATE PREPARATION

The five-year model that existed until 1951 assumed that professional education for librarianship would be built atop a liberal education in college. In its 1949 document *Training for Library Work: A Statement for Prospective Librarians Distributed to Library Schools and Inquirers*, the American Library Association said that the necessary education for a librarian included an undergraduate degree in which students acquire "considerable knowledge" of physical or social sciences, a background in history and American and English literature, at least one modern foreign language, and knowledge of research methods.[50] The statement alerted inquirers about librarianship that education for librarianship was a five-year program that included a master's degree.

The assumption that library school students would build on a broad liberal education carried over into the MLS project. As described in 1953 by Louis Shores, dean of the Florida State University Library School, "the basic education of a librarian is more than a single year of professional preparation; it is his total education before full-fledged admission to the profession, normally contained in the American system in about five years of collegiate education beyond the secondary school. These five years are approximately divided into two years of general education, two of subject concentration, and one of professional library education." Shores then quoted the new 1951 standards, which said that the library schools' programs should "be considered a unit with curriculum standards covering the entire period following secondary education." Shores argued that library education was part of an "integrated curriculum."[51]

Whether Shores's view of the standard form of undergraduate preparation was accurate or whether it was an imagined ideal is a question for research. Many contemporary commentators would have disagreed. By the 1930s, dissatisfaction with undergraduate education was widely discussed, and critics as philosophically contrary as John Dewey and Robert Hutchins agreed, as Hutchins wrote, that "the most striking fact about the higher learning in America is the confusion that besets it."[52] In his comments on Hutchins's book *The Higher Learning in America*, John Dewey described Hutchins's criticism as "trenchant" and went on to say, "The college of liberal arts is partly high school, partly university, partly general, partly special. The university consisting of graduate work for the master's and doctor's degree, and of a group of professional schools, is no better off. The universities are not only non-intellectual but they are anti-intellectual."[53]

After World War II, when the nation's attention returned to domestic affairs and when hordes of ex-GI's began enrolling in higher education, President Truman appointed the Commission on Higher Education for Democracy, which reported in 1947 that "the unity of liberal education has been splintered by overspecialization" and called for a variety of reforms, including harmonizing the demands of specialization with the need for a general education.[54] The assumptions about the state of undergraduate preparation on which Shores and other advocates of the MLS project built their case were unfounded. As Leon Carnovsky said in 1960, "one may well raise the question concerning the character of the four-year college education received by students admitted to the accredited library schools. How much of the so-called liberal education was actually vocational? We are so accustomed to equating four years of college work with a vague concept of liberal education that we ignore the actual content of the program."[55]

The assumptions that Shores and other sponsors of the MLS project made about the nature of undergraduate preparation of librarians were key components of students' preparation for librarianship as the educators understood it at the time. Librarians were to be broadly educated persons who could guide the reading of library patrons and who could provide expertise in collection development and reference assistance.

Consistently collected data on the backgrounds of new librarians are not available, but one can piece together a picture from various studies.[56] The information about the undergraduate preparation of library school students is presented in table 4.9. In the first four decades of the MLS project, enrollment of students with backgrounds in the humanities decreased, while enrollment increased of students whose undergraduate degrees were in professions such as education and business. The percentage of students with science backgrounds was consistently small throughout this period. As state regulations changed to require more teacher education preparation of school librarians, who in most states have teaching backgrounds, the percentage of library school students with education majors increased. Again, school librarians are not well represented in these data because they earn their credentials in ways other than through accredited MLS programs, but it is reasonable to assume that most school librarians, that is, the largest group of librarians, have undergraduate

Table 4.9. MLS Students' Undergraduate Majors

Majors	1947–48 %	1969 %	1980 %	1988 %
Literature	36	—	—	—
English	—	28	—	19
Humanities	—	—	45	—
Arts and humanities	—	—	—	16
History	14	17	—	11
Fine arts	2	—	—	—
Foreign languages	11	10	—	5
Library science	7	—	6	4
Professional (business and education)	—	—	16	—
Education	8	13	—	16
Business	1	—	—	3
Social sciences	8	11	24	—
Biological sciences	4	2	6	4
Physical sciences	4	5	—	3
Other	5	14	3	—
Law and medicine	—	—	—	1
Engineering	—	—	—	0.4

Note: The surveys used comparable but not identical questions; the items are grouped in an attempt to show comparable findings.
Sources: Robert R. Douglass, *The Personality of the Librarian,* doctoral dissertation, University of Chicago, 1957; Rodney F. White and David B. Macklin, *Education, Careers, and Professionalization in Librarianship and Information Science, Final Report* (Washington, D.C.: Office of Education, Bureau of Research, 1970); Association of American Library Schools, *Library Education Statistical Report,* 1980; Kathleen M. Heim and William E. Moen, *Occupational Entry: Library and Information Science Students' Attitudes, Demographics, and Aspirations Survey* (Chicago: American Library Association, 1989).

degrees in education or in a discipline or interdisciplinary program that includes preparation for teaching. The general profile of library school students that emerges in terms of undergraduate majors is contrary to the intentions of the MLS project.

An important question is whether the students who enrolled in library schools were fresh young undergraduates or were individuals employed in libraries who returned to school to acquire education so that they could be recognized as professional librarians. The Public Library Inquiry found that three-fourths of library school students had held full-time jobs in libraries prior to graduation from library school.[57] The library schools reported pertinent data only for a short time, 1956–1966, and Heim and Moen collected data in 1988, but information about prior experience in librarianship has not been part of the ALISE reports. Table 4.10 shows the percentage of MLS students new to librarianship.

Having worked as a nonprofessional employee in libraries is consistently an important factor shaping students' interests in going to library school. Ard and colleagues found in their 2006 study of one library school, and in their review of studies of other schools, that prior experience in a library was a major factor in leading people to choose librarianship as a career.[58] Libraries and library schools continue to recruit within libraries for students to attend MLS programs, among library support staffs and

Table 4.10.   MLS Students and Graduates New to Librarianship

Academic year	% new to librarianship
1949 students	25
1956–57 graduates	68
1957–58 graduates	63
1958–59 graduates	70
1959–60 graduates	57
1960–61 graduates	no data
1961–62 graduates	no data
1962–63 graduates	53
1963–64 graduates	55
1988 students	47

Sources: Robert D. Leigh, *The Public Library in the United States: The General Report of the Public Library Inquiry* (New York: Columbia University Press, 1950); AASL Statistics Committee, "The Missing Years 1956–57 and 1957–58," *Journal of Education for Librarianship* 3, no. 2 (1962): 145–58; AASL Statistics Committee, "Accredited Library School Enrollment Statistics: 1959–60," *Journal of Education for Librarianship* 4, no. 3 (1964): 169–81; AASL Statistics Committee, "Enrollment Statistics for 32 Accredited Library Schools," *Journal of Education for Librarianship* 1, no. 1 (1960): 38–46; AASL Statistics Committee, "Accredited Library School Enrollment Statistics: 1962–63," *Journal of Education for Librarianship* 5, no. 2 (1964):114–23; AASL Statistics Committee, "Accredited Library School Enrollment Statistics, 1963–64," *Journal of Education for Librarianship* 7, no. 1 (1966): 29–41; Kathleen M. Heim and William E. Moen, *Occupational Entry: Library and Information Science Students' Attitudes, Demographics, and Aspirations Survey* (Chicago: American Library Association, 1989).

among librarians who hold positions for which they do not have the MLS credential. The Institute of Museum and Library Services has funded programs of both kinds in recent years, in addition to programs to recruit individuals new to librarianship.[59] The MLS project was designed for a particular kind of student and a particular view of the needs of librarianship. By 1969, it was clear those students were not enrolling. For about the last forty years, library education has been provided to a different student, the second-career, middle-aged woman. As the generation from which librarianship has recruited moves toward retirement, the next population of students will inevitably become younger. The nature of library work will change. The times call for a revised approach to library education suited to the needs of libraries and to the needs of those who will work in them.

NOTES

1. Carolyn E. Lipscomb, "Librarian Supply and Demand," *Journal of the Medical Library Association* 91, no. 1 (2003): 7–10.

2. See, for example, Anita Hostetter's annual report "The Librarian, Board of Education for Librarianship," *ALA Bulletin*, October 1946, 366–8; *ALA Bulletin*, October 1947, 378–82; *ALA Bulletin*, October 1948, 445–7.

3. Hostetter, "The Librarian," 366.

4. "Standards for Accreditation Presented by the ALA Board of Education for Librarianship and Adopted by the ALA Council, Chicago, July 13, 1951," *ALA Bulletin*, Fall 1952, 48–49.

5. Lucy E. Fay, "An Over-All View," *College and Research Libraries* 6, no. 3 (1945): 276–8; for a similar view, see Rose Z. Marcus, "B.S. or M.S.," *Wilson Library Bulletin* 20, no. 8 (1946): 574–5.

6. Isabel Nichol, "Mid-century Trends in Education for Librarianship," *Library Journal* 75, no. 14 (1950): 1262–5.

7. Laure M. Sharp et al., *Overview of the Library Fellowship Program*, Bureau of Social Science Research, 1970, ERIC Document ED043361.

8. American Library Association, *Library Human Resources: A Study of Supply and Demand*, report prepared for the National Center for Education Statistics and the Office of Libraries and Learning Technologies by King Research (Chicago: American Library Association, 1983).

9. Richard B. Freeman, *The Over-Educated American* (New York: Academic, 1976), 60.

10. William Landram Williamson, "A Century of Students," *Library Trends* 34, no. 3 (1986): 433–49.

11. American Library Association, *Library Human Resources*.

12. ALISE *Statistical Reports* for 1991 and 2006.

13. Jennifer S. Kutzik, "Are You the Librarian?" *American Libraries* 36, no. 3 (2005): 32–34.

14. Catherine Helmick and Keith Swigger, "Core Competencies of Library Practitioners," *Public Libraries* 45, no. 2 (2006): 55–76.

15. American Library Association, *Library Human Resources*, 12.

16. U.S. Bureau of the Census, *Statistical Abstract of the United States: 2007* (Washington, D.C.: Bureau of the Census, 2006).

17. Ralph A. Beals, "Education for Librarianship," *Library Quarterly* 17, no. 4 (1947): 296–305.

18. Willard O. Mishoff, "Education for Librarianship: The Current Pattern," *Illinois Libraries*, February 1953, 74–79, 76.

19. Robert M. Hayes, *Requirements and Recommended Preparation for Entry into Programs for Professional Education in Library and Information Science*, report circulated to library school deans and directors, March 20, 1993, 10–12.

20. George A. Jeffs, *Occupational Aspiration Scale for Females*, ERIC Document ED019404.

21. Alice I. Bryan, *The Public Librarian: A Report of the Public Library Inquiry* (New York: Columbia University Press, 1952), 43.

22. Robert Raymond Douglass, *The Personality of the Librarian*, doctoral dissertation, University of Chicago, 1957, 22.

23. John Agada, "Studies of the Personality of Librarians," *Drexel Library Quarterly* 20, no. 2 (1984): 24–45.

24. Indra Mary David, *A Study of the Occupational Interests and Personality Types of Librarians*, doctoral dissertation, Wayne State University, 1990.

25. Deborah J. Grimes, "Marian the Librarian: The Truth behind the Image," in *Discovering Librarians: Profiles of a Profession*, ed. Mary Jane Scherdin (Chicago: Association of College and Research Libraries, 1994).

26. Wendi Arant and Candace R. Benefiel, eds., *The Image and Role of the Librarian* (Binghamton, N.Y.: Haworth, 2002).

27. Maura Seale, "Old Maids, Policeman, and Social Rejects: Mass Media Representations and Public Perceptions of Librarians," *Electronic Journal of Academic and Special Librarianship* 9, no. 1 (2008), http://southernlibrarianship .icaap.org.

28. Pauline Wilson, *Stereotype and Status: Librarians in the United States*, Contributions in Librarianship and Information Science 41 (Westport, Conn.: Greenwood, 1982), 153, 165.

29. American Library Association, Office of Library Personnel Resources, *Each One Reach One* (Chicago: American Library Association, 1989).

30. Studies citing the influence of librarians on student decisions include Barbara I. Dewey, "Selection of Librarianship as a Career: Implications for Recruitment," *Journal of Education for Library and Information Science* 26, no. 1 (1985): 16–24; Lois Buttlar and William Caynon, "Recruitment of Librarians into the Profession: The Minority Perspective," *Library and Information Science Research* 14, no. 3 (1992): 259–80; April Bohannon, *Anticipatory Socialization: A Study of Entering Students in Library and Information Science Programs*, doctoral dissertation, University of North Carolina at Chapel Hill, 1995; Allyson Ard et al., "Why Library and Information Science? The Results of a Career Survey of MLIS Students along with Implications for Reference Librarians and Recruitment," *Reference and Users Services Quarterly* 45, no. 3 (2006): 236–48.

31. J. Hart Walters Jr., *Image and Status of the Library and Information Services Field: Final Report* (Washington, D.C.: Office of Education, Bureau of Research, 1970), Eric Document ED 045130. Also see Howard Clayton, *An Investigation of Personality Characteristics among Library Students at One Midwestern University* (Washington, D.C.: Office of Education, Bureau of Research, 1968), Eric Document ED 024 422; and the review of literature in David, *A Study of the Occupational Interests and Personality Types of Librarians*.

32. Walters, *Image and Status of the Library and Information Services Field*.

33. Bambi Nanette Burgard, *An Examination of Psychological Characteristics and Environmental Influences of Female College Students Who Choose Traditional versus Nontraditional Academic Majors*, doctoral dissertation, University of Missouri, Kansas City, 1999, esp. 57–62.

34. Rebecca A. Watson-Boone, *A Good Match: Library Career Opportunities for Graduates of Liberal Arts Colleges* (Chicago: American Library Association, 2007).

35. Jeanine M. Williamson, Anne E. Pemberton, and John W. Lounsbury, "An Investigation of Career and Job Satisfaction in Relation to Personality Traits of Information Professionals," *Library Quarterly* 75, no. 2 (2005): 122–41.

36. Robert D. Leigh, "The Education of Librarians," in *The Public Librarian: A Report of the Public Library Inquiry*, ed. Alice I. Bryan (New York: Columbia University Press, 1952), 373, 383.

37. Douglass, *The Personality of the Librarian*.

38. Kathleen M. Heim and William E. Moen, *Occupational Entry: Library and Information Science Students' Attitudes, Demographics, and Aspirations Survey* (Chicago: American Library Association, 1989).

39. Richard Paul Bradberry, *Multi-type Undergraduate Library/Information Science Education Programs in the United States*, doctoral dissertation, University of Michigan, 1988.

40. Laure M. Sharpe, *Overview of the Library Fellowship Program* (Washington: Bureau of Social Research, 1970), 12.

41. Adele M. Fasick, "Library and Information Science Students," *Library Trends* 34, no. 4 (1986): 607–21, 616.

42. Wilson, *Stereotype and Status*, 165.

43. College Entrance Examination Board, *On Further Examination: Report of the Advisory Panel on the Scholastic Aptitude Test Score Decline* (New York: College Board, 1977).

44. Rodney F. White and David B. Macklin, *Education, Careers, and Professionalization in Library and Information Science, Final Report* (Washington, D.C.: Office of Education, Bureau of Research, 1970), Eric Document ED 054800; Heim and Moen, *Occupational Entry*.

45. For an analysis of the problem of grade inflation and a strong bibliography on the topic, see Valen E. Johnson, *Grade Inflation: A Crisis in College Education* (New York: Springer-Verlag, 2003).

46. William Landram Williamson, "A Century of Students," *Library Trends* 34, no. 3 (1986): 433–49; "Training for Library Work: A Statement for Prospective Librarians Distributed to Library Schools and Inquirers," 1949, Board of Education for Librarianship, 28/50/6, Box 4, folder Professional Education for Librarianship, 1931–56, ALA Archives.

47. Helen G. Montgomery, "The Post-35 MLS: Potential for Productive Librarianship," *Journal of Education for Librarianship* 1, no. 3 (1961): 129–40.

48. Williamson, "A Century of Students," 442.

49. ALA Office of Research and Statistics, "Age of Librarians," 2008, www.ala.org.

50. Board of Education for Librarianship, 28/50/6, Box 4, folder Professional Education for Librarianship, 1931–56, ALA Archives.

51. Louis Shores, "The Education of an American Librarian," 1953, in *Mark Hopkins' Log and Other Essays by Louis Shores*, selected by John David Marshall (Hamden, Conn.: Shoe String, 1965), 225.

52. Robert M. Hutchins, *The Higher Learning in America* (New Haven, Conn.: Yale University Press, 1936).

53. John Dewey, "President Hutchins' Proposals to Remake Higher Education," 1937, reprinted in *American Higher Education: A Documentary History*, vol. 2, ed. Richard Hofstadter and Wilson Smith (Chicago: University of Chicago Press, 1961), 949.

54. "President Truman Commission on Higher Education," in *American Higher Education Transformed, 1940–2005: Documenting the National Discourse*, ed. Wilson Smith and Thomas Bender (Baltimore: Johns Hopkins University Press, 2008), 88.

55. Leon Carnovsky, "Education for Librarianship," in *Library Development Project Reports* 4, Pacific Northwest Library Association (Seattle: University of Washington Press, 1960), quoted in C. Edward Carroll, *The Professionalization of Education for Librarianship, with Special Reference to the Years 1940–1960* (Metuchen, N.J.: Scarecrow, 1970), 84.

56. Douglass, *The Personality of the Librarian*, collected information about a broad sample of library school students at midcentury; American Association of Library Schools reported some information in 1980 in its *Library Education Statistical Report 1980* (State College, Pa.: American Association of Library Schools, 1980); Heim and Moen, *Occupational Entry*, surveyed library school students in 1988.

57. Leigh, *The Public Library*.

58. Ard et al., "Why Library and Information Science?"

59. See, for example, programs funded at the University of Tennessee, Pennsylvania Department of Education, and Texas Woman's University in 2007–2009, information about which can be found at Institute of Museum and Library Services, Awarded Grants, www.imls.gov.

5

+

Intellectual Foundations
and Library Schools

Two of the goals of the MLS project were related particularly closely. One goal was to assure a recognized distinction between training in library skills versus education in principles, theory, and management. A closely related goal was to put library school faculty in a position to develop a stronger intellectual base for librarianship. Reading the works of discussants of these topics in the 1940s and 1950s reveals an uneasiness about exactly what might fall into the category of skills and what might comprise the subjects of graduate education, as well as uneasiness about whether the library schools were in fact prepared to take on responsibility for creating and articulating an abstract apparatus that would give librarianship the intellectual coherence and respectability that it sought. It was a common assumption that developing an intellectual foundation was a responsibility of library educators, and the relocation of programs to a graduate level was seen as both a spur and an opportunity for faculty to engage the task. In adopting the MLS project, advocates argued that competencies could be learned in undergraduate programs or on the job, and the library science curricula would mature as programs that emphasized concepts and theories. The result would be a stronger base for librarians' claims to recognition as a profession.

CURRICULA

Two kinds of master's degrees have been offered in American higher education: advanced disciplinary degrees and professional degrees.

Advanced subject degree programs center on the academic disciplines, such as master's degrees in the humanities (literature, languages), sciences (physics, biology), and social sciences (political science, economics). Disciplinary master's programs presume some prior education in the discipline or in a closely related discipline. Master's degrees in the disciplines are truly advanced degrees, and the programs often presume that those who earn the degrees will eventually move onward toward a doctoral degree. The disciplinary master's degrees usually require a major focus on research. These degrees are not considered "terminal" but are stepping stones toward doctoral degrees. Professional degrees prepare students for specific occupations. They may or may not require specific preprofessional undergraduate specializations. Some professional master's degrees are offered as alternatives for those who seek to enter an occupation but did not prepare for it as undergraduates; the master of arts in teaching is an example.

Before the MLS project, there were efforts to establish the master's degree in library science as an advanced subject degree, but the project spelled the end of those. In 1926, the Graduate Library School had been established at the University of Chicago to develop people who would study librarianship, teach about it, and serve as library managers. The master's degree program at Chicago and later at similar schools such as the University of California at Berkeley was what library educators called an "advanced degree" or a "sixth-year degree," which enrolled students who had undergraduate degrees in library science and experience as librarians. When the MLS became the first professional credential, enrollment in these two-year master's programs plummeted, and by 1957 no two-year programs were being offered.[1] During the 1980s, there was much discussion of whether programs should be two-year or one-year, but the debate centered about whether one year was sufficient to teach competencies for practice, not about whether the degree itself would be an advanced degree designed to build on the knowledge acquired in a bachelor's program. The MLS project resulted in a degree that does not foster research. Few schools now require a master's thesis or a culminating research project.[2] Research requirements and experiences are concentrated at the doctoral level.

The shift to a graduate professional degree in library science was part of a broader movement in which a variety of professions moved to advance their status by associating themselves with other learned and highly credentialed groups. Until the MLS project began, library education was a four- or five-year program at the undergraduate level, with varying degrees of field experience required—the extent of the latter was always a subject of debate. In his review of events in library education leading up to the MLS project, Carl White notes that library education had an uncomfortable history in higher education because of its vocational roots. From the 1920s to the 1940s, he says, there were doubts about the appropriateness of library education as a degree program because of questions about its intellectual complexity. In the 1940s, these doubts were exacerbated in some quarters by talk of moving the program to a graduate level in hopes it would evolve. Admitting that there was a lack of confidence in the fit of library education with graduate degrees, White argues nonetheless that the MLS project was good for librarianship because it created an opportunity to develop more intellectually challenging programs. "The point we are leading up to is this," he wrote. "Universities were independent entities. Their practices varied. There was no schoolbook definition of what university education was. . . . The new movement was a groping but widely supported effort to place library education on a better footing."[3] In a similar vein, Carroll skirts the argument about whether the new degrees were of graduate level by saying, "it would appear that the distinction between *graduate study* and *professional education* has never been clear. . . . Thus, in indicating that library schools had become graduate schools by 1960, all that is implied is that they had come to be recognized in their several institutions as parts of the general grouping of graduate departments with the same admission standards, general scholastic requirements, and graduation policies as the parent institution."[4] White and Carroll artfully dodge the question of whether any content of library education changed when it moved to the graduate level, but the implication is that the curriculum simply changed course designations from undergraduate to graduate without changes in content.

Master's degrees in the MLS project were not built on the Chicago Graduate Library School model, says Carroll. Rather, they were built on the curricula of the existing five-year bachelor's degrees. The MLS project assumed that students would learn technical skills in undergraduate programs, and that the new graduate curriculum would be more advanced and theoretical. The belief was that offering courses at the graduate level would lead to courses comparable in sophistication to graduate courses in other disciplines and professions. But the curriculum stayed pretty much the same, while the credits awarded for completing it just moved up a level. The MLS project also assumed that students would come to graduate library science programs with an extensive liberal arts education.

In the debates in the 1940s, some saw the proposed new MLS degree as merely the old bachelor's degree in a new disguise. In his report on the Public Library Inquiry, Leigh described the general process among library schools as one of dropping some courses on simple technique; introducing principles and theory (which he did not describe); and collapsing several courses, such as type-of-library courses, into one, a general management course. As Leigh noted, the faculties found the squeezing difficult to accomplish, so many added a fourth quarter or a summer semester to the length of the programs.[5] What had been a fifth-year, fall/spring program became from the start a full calendar year program.

The Public Library Inquiry found that library schools in the late 1940s shared five common core areas: cataloging and classification, bibliography and reference, book selection, library administration, and the history of libraries, books, and printing. The inquiry observed that the new MLS programs, while keeping most of these areas of emphasis, would shift their foci away from technique to principle and theory. "In line with the general purpose of giving the new program a graduate-professional character suitable for accepting by university authorities for the award of the master's rather than the bachelor's degree, some simpler techniques have been dropped out of required courses," Leigh noted, and "new emphasis is placed on the principles and theory inhering in these subjects."[6] Some other changes anticipated included expansion of book selection courses from one to three or four as selection courses in major subdivisions of knowledge would be added (humanities, social sciences, physical sciences, etc.); one general management course would replace courses devoted to different types of libraries; library history would no longer be required; there would be new courses in adult education and reader guidance; and children's services in school and public libraries would be combined into one course. Recognizing the difficulty of a complete professional preparation in one academic year, it was anticipated that schools would add summer school or a fourth quarter term.[7] Notably, it was anticipated that the schools would make knowledge of basic library techniques a prerequisite for admission to graduate study and that students would acquire training in skills at the undergraduate level.

These steps were subjects of debate because "innovators," as Leigh called them, wanted to place the whole professional education experience at the graduate level and to do away with subprofessional certificate programs. Proponents of the two-step process saw the steps as ways to sharpen the distinction between professionals and subprofessionals.[8]

The changed curriculum is reflected in studies by Markey for 2000 and 2002 and Lincecum for 2007. The commonly required courses, in order of frequency, are organization of information resources, reference, foundations of library and information studies, management, research methods and evaluation, and information technology.[9] "Cataloging and classification" is a title still used in some schools, but more commonly such courses have been replaced by courses using variants of the phrases "organization of information" or "resource description." "Bibliography and reference" has been replaced by phrases that use the word "reference" but also use the term "information sources and services." "Book selection" has been replaced by "collection development." "Administration" is more commonly called "management." "History of libraries" has now been folded into "Introduction to . . . " and "Foundations . . . " courses that typically include brief historical material coupled with reviews of ethics, principles, and current issues confronting librarianship.

Two courses often required now that did not appear commonly before are information technology and research methods. Current technologies are more complex than the technologies of 1950, and they are central to library operations. However, because library school programs of study for the MLS are brief, few schools offer sequenced technology courses. Students learn about the use of various kinds of software, but they do not have an extended series of courses that would enable them to learn about the design and programming that underlie software, nor about the inner workings of hardware. Courses in research methods were implemented because some of the graduate schools require research theses or final projects. However, the thesis is often optional. In recent years, the emphasis on outcomes measurements and accountability has led to the addition of courses on research methods and evaluation. Most research methods courses in library schools are introductions to research, and although the scope of the methods these courses survey may be broad, the courses lack depth. They are generally not sequenced and do not include extensive attention to statistical or qualitative methods that underlie many different methodologies, such as surveys, historical work, or experiments. As one commentator noted in an online library discussion group, "The dirty little secret of librarianship is that most librarians take the 'no thesis' option (myself included), which means we are in a profession which claims to be expert at research, yet few of us have ever undertaken a significant research project of greater-than-one-semester scope."[10]

Most students who enter library schools do so without having engaged in any prior formal study of librarianship, so the MLS programs comprise the complete formal library education for most professional librarians. Instead of the progressive training in librarianship envisioned in 1948, with technical courses at the undergraduate level and professional courses at the master's level, the master's programs now carry the full burden of instruction in both skills and principles of librarianship. Those principles are weak in terms of social and institutional theory, focused instead on ethical principles relating to intellectual freedom and privacy. Because there is no undergraduate foundation on which to build, courses in library science are introductory. The textbooks used are comparable in content and depth to undergraduate textbooks in subjects such as management, research methods, and information technologies.

THEORY OR COMPETENCIES?

A perennial debate about professional school curricula, not only in librarianship, is whether they should focus on competencies that practitioners believe new professionals should have in order to do work, or on principles, theory, and research that underlie recognized competencies and lead to new ones. The competencies approach underlay the transition of most programs from the fifth-year model to the MLS model. Shortly after the start of the MLS project, Lester Asheim observed that the new graduate status and the strong market for graduates gave both the field of practice and the library educators an opportunity to address the question "What really is the content of librarianship?" Asheim was concerned that, in their eagerness to hire librarians equipped with immediately useful library skills, practitioners would demand, and library schools would provide, brief programs focused on the kinds of content previously taught at the undergraduate level and that a focus on principles and research would be sacrificed to the need to produce a labor force. Noting that up to 1955 practitioners had shown little interest in the research orientation exemplified by the University of Chicago Graduate Library School, Asheim said that unless the field supported schools that engaged in research for its own sake and embraced experimentation, the schools would teach only competencies and mediocrity would prevail. "In the long run," he wrote, "librarianship will get the kind of schools it deserves. It remains to be seen whether this prediction will stand as a promise or a warning."[11] Asheim argued that library schools could not develop the kind of intellectual foundations the MLS project anticipated without the support of practitioners that would enable them to lead in a more theoretical direction.

Calls for a theoretical approach to librarianship were pushed constantly through much of the twentieth century by advocates who were sympathetic with the approach taken by the Graduate Library School at the University of Chicago in its early days, but little progress could be claimed. The problems and agenda posed at the outset were unrealized but still advocated at the end of the century. Pierce Butler, a professor at Chicago, and Michael Buckland, professor at the University of California at Berkeley, made similar observations and similar arguments at the beginning and end of the period. In 1933, Butler argued for an approach to librarianship that would focus on the functions of libraries rather than on the processes that took place within libraries. He called for understanding of social science research methods broadly so that they could be applied in the instance of libraries.[12] Near the end of the century, Buckland took a similar stance. As Butler had done, he began his work with a primer on the nature of theory—implicitly, both Buckland and Butler assumed a need for such a grounding among their readers—and then went on to argue that a theory of librarianship would not be a theory relevant to libraries only but rather would be found in explanations of broader categories of human activity such as the uses of knowledge and the operations of information services generally.[13] Some, as Butler ruefully noted, had no interest in theory but believed attention should be on processes and the competencies necessary to make the processes work. Like Butler fifty years earlier, Buckland found that librarians focused more on processes within libraries, and although they had made progress refining those, they had not made progress, nor had library educators, in developing a body of theoretical knowledge. When it came to "library *science*," Buckland wrote, "there has been some progress in the past century but not very much. Because the central issues—i.e., information retrieval theory and information gathering behavior—are, or should be, rooted in truly obscure aspects of human behavior, progress will be slow and difficult and scholarly explanation will tend to lag behind the intuitive understanding of those intimately involved in the activities."[14]

The poverty of theory in librarianship has not been a problem for practicing librarians. As Butler noted in 1933, librarians have engaged in "a pragmatic quest for specific improvement rather than the adoption of a clearly conceived principle. . . . The library is conceived primarily as administering its service to individual readers."[15] Again in 1951, Butler complained that librarians' belief that librarianship is a profession "is an emotional conviction rather than a rational conclusion" because the knowledge that formed the expertise of librarianship was empirical knowledge, not theoretical knowledge.[16] He observed that a layperson could acquire the expertise of librarianship on the job, without formal education. According to Butler, the intellectual foundation that librarianship ought to develop was extensive humanistic knowledge that would lead to wisdom. He questioned the possibility of a real science of libraries and argued for using the term "librarianship" rather than "library science." His view did not prevail, however, and library science dominated as the name of the field early in the years of the MLS project. Butler's colleague Ralph Beals argued that the unique knowledge librarianship should develop was knowledge about knowledge itself. Only through an understanding of the nature of knowledge could librarians match the contents of books to the knowledge needs of readers, and only by acquiring a unique kind of knowledge could librarianship become comparable to professions like medicine, law, and engineering.[17]

The poverty of theory has been problematic for library educators when they claim librarianship's status as a discipline within academe but have difficulty demonstrating its intellectual integrity as compared to traditional academic disciplines and to other professional programs whose provenance and unique knowledge are recognized. It has been difficult not only to demonstrate that library science is a science but also to show the substantive intellectual uniqueness of course work in librarianship aside from some skills that are taught. Absence of theory also has been problematic in terms of establishing an arena of problems over which librarianship can claim responsibility and expertise as a professional group. The master's degree is an entry-level practitioner degree, however, so students want to be sure they acquire the skills that will get them a position, and employers want to be able to hire people who can perform productive work from the outset. The situation sustains the tension between educators who are sometimes perceived as wanting to teach theory and practitioners who want new librarians to have job competencies.

Another way in which absence of theory has been problematic is in terms of assessment of the value and impact of library services. Libraries report data about their activities, but the data are not always reported in relation to any particular purpose. Libraries' major data reporting has focused on how busy libraries have been, most often measured by circulation, and on their budgets and expenditures. There is a paucity of theory to describe the relationship between the roles, functions, and activities of libraries and other social institutions, or the relationship between libraries and individuals. Theoretical models of the interactions of variables that relate to library services would, conceivably, lead to predictions of results of different models of practice and, where those results were not obtained, might lead to reconsideration of models. Absent such models, assessment of outcomes in the contemporary environment is based on narratives, compelling stories, and nebulous descriptions of changes in patrons' lives or intangible benefits to patrons. Assessment has focused more on justifying funding and attracting additional funding than on demonstration of accomplishment of specific missions and purposes.

While lamentations about the absence of theory abound in the library literature, so do complaints that the library school curricula do not adequately teach professional competencies. The competency approach was a topic of much discussion in library education in the 1980s. After most schools with accredited masters programs closed their undergraduate programs in library science, some librarians and library educators tried to move the schools toward competency approaches. However, the competency approach to library education was challenged by shifts in the ideology of accreditation, which provided schools with an alternative to prescriptions for curricula. The ideology of accreditation for the last twenty-five years has focused on institutional goals and outcomes, rather than on particular content of academic programs or on resources that are required to educate students in some particular content. Advocates of a competency approach to library education have been challenged by this emphasis on institutional goals in accreditation processes, particularly since the adoption of the 1992 *ALA Standards for Accreditation*. The 1992 standards set aside a competency-based approach in favor of an approach based on assessment of goals, a particular kind of planning process, and measurements of effectiveness. The 2008 revision of the standards strengthened the emphasis on assessment and planning. The 1992 and 2008 standards reflect a broad movement in higher education accreditation.

Despite the ALA standards, however, the advocates for an approach to library education based on competencies remain vocal. An effort to specify competencies for graduates of ALA-accredited programs was one outcome of the first ALA Congress on Professional Education in 1999. Following the meeting, the ALA Executive Board created four task forces, including the Task Force on Core Competencies and Generalist of the Future.[18] The task force produced a draft statement, "Core Competencies for Librarians," in 2001, but that languished for years before being taken up by a new group in 2007, when ALA President Leslie Burger appointed the ALA Presidential Task Force on Library Education.[19] In 2008, this new task force produced "Core Competencies of Librarianship," which was adopted by the ALA Council in January 2009.[20]

The competencies statement approved by the ALA in 2009 would be familiar to librarians of 1950. It presents general statements of what new graduates of accredited programs should know, organized in familiar categories: foundations of the profession, information resources, organization of recorded knowledge and information, technological knowledge and skills, reference and user services, research, continuing education and lifelong learning, and administration and management. There have been changes in curricula and in expectations of graduates, but the focus of required courses and proposed standards still appears to be on the management of institutions that provide knowledge records for social groups through the application of expertise in selection, organization, and response to clients' inquiries. The competencies are grouped, but they are neither ranked in importance nor sequenced in terms of development of learning. Whether it is more important to be able to catalog a book, teach information literacy, manage a room, or make a digital collection is not addressed.

In their critiques of intellectual foundations of librarianship, both Butler and Buckland noted that librarians and library educators devoted considerable attention to values and ethical principles, an emphasis that had a strong impact on the model of professionalism adopted by librarians. The emphasis survives in the 2009 ALA competency document, which includes a number of statements that prescribe attitudes or beliefs rather than competencies. For example, the competency policy says that a person graduating from an ALA-accredited master's program in library and information studies "should know and, where appropriate, be able to employ" the following:

- The ethics, values, and foundational principles of the library and information profession.
- The role of library and information professionals in the promotion of democratic principles, intellectual freedom, and diversity of thought.
- The importance of effective advocacy for libraries, librarians, other library workers, and library services.

American librarianship devotes itself to social causes and to values that are related to practice, to the extent that holding what are considered appropriate beliefs and adhering to an approved ideology have become confounded with professional skills and knowledge. A plethora of ALA policy documents detail what librarians should believe.

A compilation of competency statements from a variety of ALA divisions and other library associations reveals the importance that competencies have established over theory in librarianship. The *Competency Index for the Library Field* is "a compilation of competency statements that address a broad spectrum of library practice and service."[21] The document mentions theories seven times, and six of these instances refer to a theory from another profession or discipline: "Understands and applies marketing theory and practices, . . . Understands and applies knowledge of adult learning theory, . . . Understands the theory of appeal, . . . Understands the theory, processes, standards and best practices of digital creation, management, storage and preservation, . . . Develops and delivers training events, following principles of learning theory and interactivity, . . . Understands the theories of reading development for children (including early and emergent literacy) and the reading curriculum used by community schools, . . . Understands the theories of reading development for young adults." One mention of theory—"Understands the theory, processes, standards and best practices of digital creation, management, storage and preservation"—suggests that there is a theory of digital management, storage, and preservation, but it is difficult to imagine what such a theory would be. Sometimes librarians use the word "theory" to include any reason for doing some particular thing.

The *Competency Index* also identifies "principles" in the various competency statements. These include the basic principles of marketing, managing organizational change, project management, instructional design, adult learning, usability and accessibility, project management, identity management (for record keeping, not psychology), and user ID and account management. As in the case of theory, all of these are principles derived from other professions and disciplines. The knowledge or skill sets identified in the competency index that are based on theories or principles are not unique to librarianship nor were they developed within library science.

Attempts to dress up librarianship by developing a body of theory were doomed from the start, partly because, as Bonnie Nelson puts it, "The goal seems to be not to develop theory for the sake of advancing library work, but for the sake of passing the attribute test for professionalism."[22] The effort showed failure to appreciate that there are different kinds of professions. Librarianship could not emulate the learned professions because it is an organizational profession, practiced through institutions. It was not reasonable to expect that there could be a "science" of libraries distinct from a science of all bureaucracies and organizations. The effort assumed there was a need for theory in order for librarianship to have its own specialized knowledge, but not all specialized knowledge requires a unique body of theory.

CURRICULA AND INFORMATION SCIENCE

Some library educators sought to move library education toward theory by subsuming library science within the rubric of information science, a trend that emerged in the 1980s. There is considerable confusion about the differences between library science and information science, and there is an enormous amount of literature on the topic.[23] Some argued that information science was a subset of library science, with its roots in indexing and documentation, while others argued that library science was a subset of information science because librarianship is but one of many institutional and professional approaches to dealing with the overarching phenomenon of information. Information science is perceived as more oriented to computer technology, perhaps because there is a popular confusion of science and technology. Some see the distinction as merely a marketing ploy which recognizes that information science is more glamorous than library science. Librarian Michael Gorman has often delighted librarians and needled information scientists by saying, "Information science is library science for men,"[24] but even leaders in information science have expressed their own dissatisfaction with the field. Marcia Bates described the insecurity of the information disciplines, complaining that they received respect belatedly and that even though they are now recognized, confusion reigns about exactly what the field is:

Any of us who have taught in universities in the information disciplines have been patronized and dismissed by the more established disciplines more times than we can count. We have been treated as the astrologers and phrenologists of modern science—assumed to be desperately trying to cobble together the look of scholarship in what are surely trivial and nearly content-free disciplines. We have been parked at the margins of the university, along with the family science (formerly home economics), recreation studies, and physical education departments. . . . Now, almost overnight, in the late twentieth and early twenty-first century, the information sciences have exploded into scientific and social validity. . . . Ironically, however, that legitimacy has often been gained without much clarity on just what the information disciplines are about."[25]

The confusion about and between information science and library science and whether the emphasis on information science in some schools has served librarianship well are topics too large to treat adequately here. Suffice it to say, the matter is confused, and some would say the schools have deliberately confused it. The information science schools seem to want to maintain the status associated with ALA accreditation while achieving whatever benefits may be associated with an information science degree. There is much contention on this matter. As one dean remarked in confidence, "The dirty secret of our IS master's program is that the majority of the enrollment is people who want to be school librarians, so school librarians pay the bills to support the IS program." To distinguish themselves from library schools, a group of schools banded together as the iSchools Caucus. Fifteen of the nineteen members are schools that offer degrees accredited by the American Library Association.[26] These schools consider themselves unlike "library schools," but they continue to maintain the library association's accreditation.

The way accrediting works in librarianship contributes to the confusion about library science and information science. As their degrees came up for renewal of accreditation under the 1992 ALA standards, some library schools presented their information science degrees for ALA accreditation. They were able to do that because the standards emphasized institutional goals and processes, not program content. The University of North Texas was the first university to achieve ALA accreditation of its master of information science degree in 1992. Other universities followed, changing the names of their degrees from library science to information science but still seeking ALA accreditation of their degrees.

Confusion remains concerning which programs are library science programs and which are information science programs, and what ALA accreditation actually means in terms of content. ALA accreditation under the 1992 and 2008 standards is based on a model in which individual schools set individual goals and then are assessed in terms of their planning processes and their accomplishments related to their individual goals. The degrees accredited are degrees in "library and information studies," which the 2008 standards explain as encompassing "information and knowledge creation, communication, identification, selection, acquisition, organization and description, storage and retrieval, preservation, analysis, interpretation, evaluation, synthesis, dissemination, and management."[27] There is no clear requirement that a school with a degree accredited by the library association in fact offer a specific kind of degree, only a specific level of degree.

The resurgence of undergraduate programs in schools that also have ALA accredited master's degrees has been in information science programs, not library science. Most undergraduate programs in library science have disappeared. Sixteen schools with accredited masters programs offer undergraduate programs, but the majority of these are in the area of information science, with only a few offering a bachelor's degree in library science.[28] Undergraduate enrollment in library science programs bottomed in 1984 and did not recover. Undergraduate activity has revived in information science programs. Some schools that have ALA-accredited master's degrees also offer undergraduate programs in information science or information studies, but there is little activity in library science at the bachelor's degree level (see table 5.1).

Table 5.1. Bachelor's Degrees Awarded

Year awarded	BS degrees	Number of schools awarding degrees
1984	64	7
1985	300	8
1986	217	5
1987	235	7
1988	174	7
1989	163	8
1990	112	6
1991	83	6
1992	78	7
1993	110	6
1994	219	9
1995	97	5
1996	181	6
1997	218	9
1998	280	10
1999	366	11
2000	604	13
2001	611	15
2002	871	12
2003	1037	16
2004	1010	12
2005	1005	17

Source: Association for Library and Information Science Education, *Statistical Report,* 1985–2006.

Most of the undergraduate enrollment is at four information science schools: Drexel University, University of Pittsburgh, Syracuse University, and Florida State University. The annual statistics report of the Association for Library and Information Science Education (ALISE) tracks this activity, but again, these are not called library science programs. The National Center for Education Statistics identified nine colleges or universities that offered bachelor's degree programs in library science in 2009, three of which are at universities that also offer ALA-accredited master's degree programs. Thirty-four colleges offer associate degrees in library science.[29]

LIBRARY SCHOOLS IN UNIVERSITIES

The MLS project placed many of its hopes on the leadership the library schools would provide once they had enhanced status as graduate programs. In his review of library education as it stood in 1948–1949, Robert Leigh found positive changes had occurred since the last major report on the topic, Charles C. Williamson's *Training for Library Service*, published by the Carnegie Corporation in 1923.[30] In the forthcoming changes due to the new accreditation standards, Leigh saw indications that library schools would continue to become stronger as components within universities, and in fact they did, although their course has not been smooth. Their increased strength may be attributed in part to the near monopoly the schools with accredited programs had on library education, to growth in federal funding, to their status as graduate programs, and to changes in universities that made universities more like library schools just as library schools were trying to become more like the rest of the university.

The enrollment bubble of the 1960s led to creation of more library schools than were viable. The number of schools with accredited programs peaked at 71 in 1978; in 2008, there were 57 schools with ALA accredited programs, 7 of which were in Canada. The enrollment crash in the 1970s led to closings of library schools and sharp competition among those that survived. Librarians and library educators were rattled in the 1980s and 1990s by the closure of so many library schools, especially the eminent schools at Case Western Reserve University (closed 1987), University of Denver (closed in 1987, reopened, then reaccredited in 2003), Emory University (closed 1988), University of Chicago (closed 1990), and Columbia University (closed 1992), and the withdrawal from ALA accreditation by the University of California at Berkeley in 1994.[31] Termination of these programs led to nervousness among librarians about the schools on which they relied for employees and to defensiveness among library school deans and directors about the soundness of their institutions.

Responding to anxiety about their future, library schools and university administrations implemented practical measures in attempting to assure that the schools could deliver consistently on the performance measures that make for component success with universities: innovative academic programs, strong enrollment, and acquisition of external funding. Many schools were strengthened by receiving grants under the Title II-B program of the Higher Education Act, which channeled millions of dollars into library education from 1965 to 1995, followed by strong funding through the Institute of Museum and Library Services initiated during the George W. Bush administration. Schools engaged in enrollment strategies such as distance learning to make themselves valuable economic producers for their universities. About a third of the library education programs in recent years experienced reductions in status and autonomy within their own institutions as the administrative units in which the programs reside have seen their deanships changed to positions as directors or department chairs and their place on the university organization chart subordinated to larger units. This was the case, for example, at the University of California at Los Angeles and the State University of New York at Buffalo.[32] Some library schools became hybrid units, melding information science, teacher education, or communications programs, joining library education with the programs and terminologies that appeal to university administrators and external constituents. One cost has been the dedication of vast amounts of effort to institutional survival rather than to a broader academic purpose. According to Richard Cox, "In buying into their parent institutions' moneymaking mission, many library schools have lost their moorings. . . . We've made a pact with the devil by furthering these bottom-line goals."[33]

One of Leigh's concerns about the schools in 1948–1949 was that the faculties were small and staffed with too many part-time rather than full-time instructors, an issue that persists. There were 220 library school faculty members in 1948–1949, 58 percent of whom were part-time employees. To enable library schools to fulfill their multiple roles in teaching, research, and service, and to have high standing in their universities, Leigh contended that larger faculties made up of more full-time employees were needed. Table 5.2 shows faculty composition in terms of full-time and part-time members for selected years between 1948 and 2005. In the early years of the MLS project, library school faculties grew as hoped, reducing both the ratio of students to faculty and the percentage of part-time faculty. The nadir of enrollment in 1980 was also the time of lowest use of part-time faculty and the lowest student/faculty ratio. After 1980, these two trends reversed. Now the use of part-time faculty is even higher than in 1948, and the student/faculty ratio has nearly doubled since 1980.[34]

Table 5.2. Library School Faculty Members, Full Time and Part Time

	1948	1960	1971	1980	1990	2000	2005
Full time	92	162	656	707	621	695	835
% full time	42	57	67	72	60	52	47
Part time	128	120	324	277	406	586	937
% part time	58	42	33	28	40	48	53
Total faculty	220	282	980	984	1027	1281	1772
Total FTE	133	202	737	784	727	872	1102
Mean full time	3	5	12	10	11	12	15
Mean part time	4	4	6	4	7	10	17
Enrollment	2064	3263	10,275	8770	11,020	13,127	18,271
Ratio of students to full time faculty	22/1	20/1	16/1	12/1	18/1	19/1	22/1

FTE = full-time equivalent
Sources: C. Edward Carroll, The Professionalization of Education for Librarianship (Metuchen, N.J.: Scare-crow, 1970); American Library Association Committee on Accreditation, Statistical Data from Annual Review Reports 1971–77; Association for Library and Information Science Education, Statistical Reports, 1982, 1992, 2002, 2006.

In 1948, the student/faculty ratio and the number of part-time faculty distinguished library school faculty from the faculties of higher-status disciplines. The present situation is different. The American Association of University Professors (AAUP) reported a steady rise of persons in contingent faculty status from 1975 to 2003 and a corresponding decline in full-time tenured and tenure-track positions (contingent faculty hold part-time or full-time, non-tenure track positions). Nationally, full-time tenured positions declined from 36 percent of positions in 1975 to 24 percent in 2003, and tenure-track positions declined from 20 percent to 11 percent. Contingent positions rose from 33 percent of persons holding positions in 1975 to 65 percent in 2003.[35] The percentage of faculty who are part-time does not represent the full portion of contingent faculty, because some full-time faculty hold annual appointments rather than tenured or tenure-track appointments.

The status of library schools within their own institutions has been a continuing concern of library educators and librarians. A relevant question about library education is the extent to which library schools' faculties are contingent and whether conditions in library schools are similar to those in their home institutions. Data from the 2004 ALISE Statistical Report are comparable to the data presented by AAUP; the data in the 2004 report describe the situation in schools in fall 2003.[36] The average percentage of contingent faculty in American universities offering ALA-accredited degrees is 44 percent; the average for those institutions' library schools is 42 percent. The difference in institutional and library school mean numbers of contingent faculty is not significant. The median percent of contingent faculty is 38 percent for library schools and 40 percent for their universities. The universities that are homes to library schools that offer ALA-accredited programs are less populated by contingent faculty than are postsecondary institutions in general.

Instead of library schools becoming more like universities by increasing the percentage of full-time faculty, universities have become more like library schools were in 1948 by employing more and more part-time faculty. There is a difference between library schools and iSchools in size of faculties. The mean number of full-time faculty in the United States was 24 at iSchools in 2005 and 15 for all schools; the mean number of part-time faculty was 29 (55 percent of faculty) but 17 for all schools (53 percent of faculty).[37]

CHANGES IN HIGHER EDUCATION

The altered composition of higher education faculties was not anticipated in 1950, and it is but one of several unforeseen developments that impacted the MLS project. Some other broad changes in higher education after 1950 made some of the assumptions underlying the MLS project invalid. Colleges and their students have changed greatly. In addition to changes in faculty composition, four other changes are of particular importance for library education. First, graduation from college is much more common now than it was in 1950, so the status and prestige associated with bachelor's and higher degrees is shared much more broadly: 6 percent of individuals over age twenty-four held bachelor's or higher degrees in 1950, whereas 28 percent held degrees in 2006.[38] That change is positive for society, but insofar as the MLS project relied on the exclusivity that was associated with having completed higher education in 1950, it has been undercut by increased participation in college and graduate school.

A second change in higher education is that college has become a vocational program for most students; a college education is neither geared to nor sought for a general education. Students go to college so they will earn more, and they do: the median income for a college graduate in 2006 was $50,900.[39] That is only slightly less than what professional librarians with MLS degrees earned in 2006 ($52,744). The liberal arts experience that MLS project proponents assumed as a foundation for a career in librarianship is now a minority experience. Public policy focuses on preparation for the workforce, standardization of curricula, transferability of credits, and accountability.

A third change is a decline in adequacy of students' preparation for college and in their academic performance in college and their accomplishment as college graduates. In 2006, the secretary of education's Commission on the Future of Higher Education, known as the Spellings Commission for then Secretary Margaret Spellings, noted that "the percentage of college graduates deemed proficient in prose literacy has actually declined from 40 to 31 percent in the past decade."[40] The liberally educated, intellectually ready students that library educators counted on as a recruiting pool for librarianship is not deep.

A fourth change is in the duration of undergraduate experiences. According to the Spellings Commission in 2006, only 66 percent of college students complete bachelor's degrees in less than six years. The mean time even for those who do not interrupt their studies is more than five years. Add another two or three years to that for library school, and the investment in education becomes seven or eight years, not the five years envisioned in 1950.

Contemporary college students are different from students of 1950: they are older, they go to college part time, and they are less likely to go away to college. According to the Spellings Commission, change in higher education "will need to take account of the new realities that are sometimes overlooked in public discussions about the future of higher education. While many Americans still envision the typical undergraduate as an 18- to 22-year-old with a recently acquired high school diploma attending classes at a four-year institution, the facts are more complex. Of the nation's nearly 14 million undergraduates, more than four in ten attend two-year community colleges. Nearly one-third are older than 24 years old. Forty percent are enrolled part-time."[41]

THE COST OF LIBRARY EDUCATION TO LIBRARIANS

One of the factors not discussed in the design of the MLS project was the cost to students. Since many of its advocates in the 1940s saw the year required to complete an MLS as simply a replacement for the fifth year of a five-year bachelor's degree, it seems to have been assumed that the cost to students would be a wash. The length of programs would not be extended, but students would get a master's degree for that fifth year instead of a bachelor's degree. However, the outcome has been different, and for students seeking degrees, the cost has been considerably higher in several respects. The costs of a master's degree include not only extension of study beyond four years but also higher tuition and fees for graduate students.

The calculated total cost for tuition and fees for accredited master's degrees in library science in 2004, the most recent year for which data are available, was about $100 million (see table 5.3). The ALISE annual

Table 5.3. Costs of Master of Library Science Degrees, 2004–2005

School	In-state ncosts	Out-of-state costs	% in-state	% out-of-state	In state total	Out-of-state total
Alabama	78	9,260	25,328	86	14	620,439	278,557
Albany	110	10,350	16,380	86	14	981,387	248,648
Arizona	93	11,592	34,236	79	21	850,586	671,813
Buffalo	142	12,624	18,024	96	4	172,2696	99,817
UCLA	77	9,479	22,418	92	8	674,412	131,190
Catholic	85	37,195	37,195	16	84	496,367	2,665,208
Clarion	76	11,972	17,842	80	20	725,168	275,266
Denver	27	20,938	20,938	100	0	565,326	0
Dominican	186	21,780	21,780	97	3	391,7394	133,686
Drexel	95	34,800	34,800	48	52	158,3574	1,702,590
Emporia	87	7,032	19,768	48	49	290,597	842,710
Florida State	153	7,693	28,385	61	39	720,342	1,685,047
Hawaii	53						
Illinois	192	11,637	59,081	65	35	1,459,001	3,936,213
Indiana	189	8,489	24,728	75	25	1,209,733	1,149,704
Iowa	29	12,364	33,332	79	21	282,542	204,925
Kent State	236	10,980	20,628	98	2	2,549,820	77,891
Kentucky	103			88	12		
Long Island	192	25,380	25,380	92	7	4,502,615	360,599
La State	75	9,387	24,687	83	17	585,045	312,908
Maryland	119	15,110	27,998	74	26	1,321,596	882,917
Michigan	137	27,171	54,579	41	59	1,529,917	4,404,143
Missouri	79	10,680	27,581	74	26	623,509	568,693
NC Central	88			86	14		
NC Chapel Hill	73	9,302	35,798	65	35	442,059	912,026
NC Greensboro	104	8,644	30,744	95	5	854,027	159,869
North Texas	249	14,324	23,612	74	26	2,639,340	1,528,641
Oklahoma	61	8,422	19,535	97	3	498,843	34,557
Pittsburgh	185	6,385	13,058	73	27	862,294	652,247
Pratt	116	24,300	24,300	81	19	2,277,590	54,1210
Puerto Rico	19	3,045	0	100	0	57,855	0
Queens	142	8,280	15,300	98	2	1,147,542	52,142
Rhode Island	74	12,563	33,725	53	47	492,721	1,172,956
Rutgers	164	16,259	23,313	86	12	2,303,835	454,977
St. John's	40	27,220	27,220	92	8	1,007,140	81,660
San Jose	316	7,854	9,030	97	3	2,399,962	88,458
Simmons	299	27,000	27,000	85	15	6,837,831	1,235,169
S. Carolina	139	3,445	7,460	66	34	315,087	354,633
S. Florida	158	9,090	34,888	96	4	1,377,335	226,004
S. Conn.	89	9,444	16,826	54	46	454,719	681,369
S. Miss.	39	8,424	18,993	54	44	178,067	324,438
Syracuse	77	29,016	29,016	100	22	34,232	
Tennessee	77	12,222	35,070	68	32	639,944	864,125
Texas	112	10,729	22,694	67	33	807,507	833,687
Tx. Woman's	196	6,772	16,060	75	25	996,811	783,792
Washington	208	16,236	36,636	70	30	2,360,585	2,293,707
Wayne State	202	11,326	23,717	96	4	2,189,474	206,006
Wis. Madison	64	18,535	52,895	72	28	856,465	941,108
Wis. Milw.	105	16,262	44,994	58	42	983,526	2,003,133
						$62,426,860	$37,058,438

Total cost of U.S. MLS 2004–2005: $99,485,297

Note: Data for degree costs as of fall 2004 are reported in the ALISE *Statistical Report* for 2005; numbers of graduates in 2004–2005 are reported in the ALISE Statistical Report for 2006. The estimated total cost of degrees was computed by summing the products of the cost of a degree times the number of graduates times the percentage of the student body reported by each school as either in-state or out-of-state residents. Canadian schools were excluded in the total. The method assumes that the proportion of students graduating is the same as the overall proportion of students that is either in-state or out-of-state; schools do not report the proportion of graduates by residence status. The University of Hawaii, University of Kentucky, and North Carolina Central University did not report the data needed to make the calculation. Had those schools been included, with their 254 graduates, the total would have been over $100 million.

statistical reports list the total cost for tuition and fees of MLS degrees by school; schools are asked to report the cost separately for in-state and out-of-state students. Schools also report the percentage of students who are state residents and nonstate residents. The calculated cost is a conservative estimate. Data for graduates in 2004–2005 are reported in the ALISE *Statistical Report for 2006*.[42]

Since 2004, tuition and fees have risen, along with other costs; within one year, in-state tuition in the U.S. schools had increased by 7 percent and nonresident costs by 5.4 percent.[43] Inflation takes its toll: in 2008 dollars, the cost of those 2004 degrees was over $118 million. The total cost of library education would be much higher if one also were to factor in the opportunity costs—the amount of salary the students might have earned if they had been employed instead of attending school—and the real costs to students that schools cannot calculate or report, such as child care costs, purchase of computers and network access, books, and travel. The whole amount does not come from students' pockets, because many students receive scholarships or tuition discounts, but the money does come from somewhere in society. If students had been able to earn credentials to become librarians during their undergraduate programs, most of that $100 million could have been spent for something else. Moreover, there has been a steady decline in completion rates of those who start library education programs (as shown in table 5.2). That means a lot of students have made an investment in programs from which they did not graduate. The schools do not report retention-to-degree rates in the ALISE *Statistical Reports*, but clearly the ratio of graduates to number of enrollments has declined steadily.

Beyond the cost to students, the total cost of library education would include the universities' costs (physical and administrative infrastructure, faculty salaries, etc.), but extracting the portion of library education costs from such variables as the cost of library services or campus heating is beyond the scope of this work. Library education also has costs for library associations.

NOTES

1. C. Edward Carroll, *The Professionalization of Education for Librarianship, with Special Reference to the Years 1940–1960* (Metuchen, .N.J: Scarecrow, 1970).
2. Jean-Pierre V. M. He'rubel , "Contextual Culture of the Master's Degree and the Decline of the M.L.S. Thesis: An Exploratory Review Essay," *Libraries and Culture* 40, no. 1 (2005): 63–84.
3. Carl M. White, *A Historical Introduction to Library Education: Problems and Progress to 1951* (Metuchen, N.J.: Scarecrow, 1976), 254.
4. Carroll, *The Professionalization of Education for Librarianship*, 220–1.

5. Robert D. Leigh, *The Public Library in the United States: The General Report of the Public Library Inquiry* (New York: Columbia University Press, 1950).

6. Leigh, *The Public Library*, 215.

7. Leigh, *The Public Library*, 216.

8. Leigh, *The Public Library*, 218.

9. Karen Markey, "Current Educational Trends in the Information and Library Science Curriculum," *Journal of Education for Library and Information Science* 45, no. 4 (2004): 317–39; Taylor Lincecum, "Lengths of Accredited MLS Programs," unpublished report prepared for Texas Woman's University School of Library and Information Studies Curriculum Committee, January 2008.

10. Sharon McCaslin, post to COLLIB discussion group, August 12, 2009.

11. Lester Asheim, "Education for Librarianship," *Library Quarterly* 25, no. 1 (1955): 76–90.

12. Pierce Butler, *An Introduction to Library Science* (Chicago: University of Chicago Press, 1933), chap. 5.

13. Michael K. Buckland, *Library Services in Theory and Context*, 2nd ed. (New York: Pergamon, 1988).

14. Michael K. Buckland, "Education for Librarianship in the Next Century," *Library Trends* 34, no. 4 (1986): 777–88, 783.

15. Butler, *An Introduction to Library Science*, 114.

16. Pierce Butler, "Librarianship as a Profession," *Library Quarterly* 21, no. 4 (1951): 235–247, 237.

17. Ralph Beals, "Education for Librarianship," *Library Quarterly* 17, no. 4 (1947): 296–305.

18. "Professional Education Task Forces Established," *Prism* 8, no. 1 (2000): 1.

19. John H. Berry, "Old Debates Renew Libraries," *Library Journal*, September 1, 2007, 8.

20. American Library Association, "Core Competences of Librarianship, Approved and Adopted as Policy by the ALA Council, January 27, 2009," www.ala .org.

21. Beth Gutsche, ed., *Competency Index for the Library Field*, Compiled by WebJunction, 2009, www.webjunction.org.

22. Bonnie R. Nelson, "The Chimera of Professionalism," *Library Journal*, October 1, 1980, 2029–2033, 2030.

23. For a discussion of the background of the distinction, see Margaret F. Stieg, *Change and Challenge in Library and Information Science Education* (Chicago: American Library Association, 1992).

24. Michael Gorman, "Cataloging, Chaos, and Computers," Lillian E. Bradshaw Lecture, Texas Woman's University School of Library and Information Studies, 1997.

25. M. J. Bates, "Defining the Information Disciplines in Encyclopedia Development," *Information Research* 12, no. 4 (2007), http://InformationR.net.

26. iSchools Caucus, "Who Are the iSchools?" 2008, www.ischools.org.

27. American Library Association, Committee on Accreditation, *Standards of Accreditation for Programs in Library and Information Studies* (Chicago: American Library Association, 2008), 3.

28. Colin Koteles and Carolyn Haythornthwaite, "Undergraduate Programs in Information Science: A Survey of Requirements and Goals," *Journal of Education for Library and Information Science* 43, no. 2 (2002): 144–54.

29. National Center for Education Statistics, College Navigator, http://nces .ed.gov.

30. Robert D. Leigh, "The Education of Librarians," in *The Public Librarian: A Report of the Public Library Inquiry*, ed. Alice I. Bryan (New York: Columbia University Press, 1952), 299–428; Charles C. Williamson, *Training for Library Service* (New York: Carnegie Corp., 1923).

31. American Library Association, "Accredited Library and Information Studies Master's Programs from 1925 through Present," www.ala.org.

32. Charles R. Hildreth, "Organizational Realignment of LIS Programs in Academia: From Independent Standalone Units to Incorporated Programs," *Journal of Education for Library and Information Science* 43, no. 2 (2002): 126.

33. Richard J. Cox, "Why Survival Is Not Enough," *American Libraries* 37, no. 6 (2006): 42–44, 43.

34. Data collected from Leigh, "Education of Librarians," and from ALISE, *Library and Information Science Statistical Report, 2005*. FTE faculty were computed by adding the number of full-time faculty to one-third the number of part-time faculty. Schools compute FTE variously; some count a part-time person as one-quarter FTE, which would reduce the number of total FTEs to 1027.

35. American Association of University Professors, *AAUP Contingent Faculty Index 2006*, www.aaup.org.

36. Association for Library and Information Science Education, *Statistical Report 2004*, www.alise.org.

37. ALISE, *Statistical Report 2006*, tables I-41, I-43, www.alise.org.

38. Sandy Baum and Jennifer Ma, *Education Pays 2007: The Benefits of Higher Education for Individuals and Society*, Trends in Higher Education Series, College Board, 2007, www.collegeboard.com.

39. Baum and Ma, *Education Pays 2007*.

40. U.S. Department of Education, *A Test of Leadership: Charting the Future of U.S. Higher Education*, 2006, www.ed.gov.

41. U.S. Department of Education, *A Test of Leadership*.

42. The ALISE *Statistical Report for 2006* did not include data on percentages of in-state and out-of-state residency status of students.

43. Calculated from tuition and fees tables II-13 in ALISE *Statistical Report* for 2005 and 2006.

6

✛

Librarians' Work

Differentiating between professional librarians and other library employees was seen as a necessary step toward overall improvements for librarians. The Public Library Inquiry found that most of the work done in libraries was not professional but rather technical or clerical. An ALA task force in 2001 observed that the public is often unable to distinguish between librarians and support staff, so the status of librarianship suffers because the public most often observes the people doing the nonprofessional work and thinks of them as librarians.[1] The percentage of librarians holding appropriate academic credentials rose between 1949 and 2003, but other problems cited in the Public Library Inquiry remain. Only a small portion of the people who are employed in public libraries can claim the title "librarian" as defined by the ALA; 82.6 percent of the staff of public libraries do not have an MLS degree.[2]

RECOGNITION OF THE MLS

The MLS project specified an accredited academic credential for librarians. Advocates of the project did not stop with the change in accreditation requirements, however. Having won that battle, they then pushed to redefine librarianship itself by making the newly accredited degree central to the definition of "librarian." They had to win recognition by two groups: librarians themselves and society at large. Winning over librarians involved education and policy making mostly within the ALA.

Winning social recognition required both public relations work and lobbying legislators.

The 1951 accreditation standards set the master's degree as the only degree to be accredited, but the standards did not address the definition of
"librarian." Acceptance within librarianship of a definition based on the
credential took several decades, a process moved along incrementally by
its advocates so that librarians who had been educated prior to the 1951
standards would not feel alienated by the new definition. Lester Asheim
was a leading proponent of differentiating between librarians and others who worked in libraries. Asheim had been a student of Pierce Butler
at the University of Chicago. It was Butler who in 1933 posited three
kinds of librarians: professional librarians who had generalized scientific
knowledge, technical library workers who were trained in operating the
apparatus of the library, and clerks who had skills in particular library
processes.[3] Asheim had been dean of the Graduate Library School at the
University of Chicago from 1952 to 1961, then served as director of international relations at the ALA before becoming the first director of the
ALA Office for Library Education, holding that post from 1966 to 1971.
The Office of Library Education later became the Office of Accreditation.
Asheim moved the agenda of differentiation along through his activities in the ALA, such as convening a conference on "Library Manpower
Needs and Utilization" in 1967. Asheim defined the problem and set the
agenda for the invitational conference, which produced recommendations
calling for a "spectrum of training and education" for persons employed
in libraries. The recommendations called for a task analysis that would
lead to a redefinition of jobs and would structure the functions, responsibilities, and rewards of library personnel.[4] The objective was to define
librarianship in such a way that librarians would no longer do work that
was not consistent with the status they sought.

After several years of discussion, in 1970 the ALA Council adopted
a policy statement entitled "Library Education and Manpower" that
described categories of library work and levels of education and training appropriate to each category.[5] The council distinguished between
librarians and others who worked in libraries on the basis of categories
of responsibilities, and it said that the appropriate level of education for
a professional librarian was a master's degree in library science or some
other appropriate field. The policy did not address the status of holders
of the old five-year bachelor's degrees, and in responding to questions,
Asheim argued that the policy should be seen not as detrimental to
any librarian but as a policy that "describes objectives toward which to
strive."[6] The discussion about formally distinguishing between librarians and nonprofessional library staff on the basis of degrees continued
for over a decade. Some who thought of themselves as librarians took

offense at being redefined as nonlibrarians, while others saw an explicit policy as a way to address the status problem that had dogged librarians for a century. The policy was revised in 1976 and renamed "Library Education and Personnel Utilization," then revised again in 2002 and adopted by the ALA Council as the "Library and Information Studies and Human Resource Utilization Policy Statement." The policy says that the "basic requirement" for inclusion in the category "professional personnel" is a master's degree. Employees who do not have a master's degree are considered "supportive personnel." The *ALA Policy Manual* says, "The master's degree from a program accredited by the American Library Association (or from a master's level program in library and information studies accredited or recognized by the appropriate national body of another country) is the appropriate professional degree for librarians."[7]

The ALA's personnel policy never had the force of work rules because librarianship is too decentralized for such a result to be possible, nor was it intended to serve that function. The policy was an attempt to clarify how the education acquired in the process of earning an MLS prepared librarians for work that differed from the work of others employed in libraries. It served more as a rationale for the MLS than as a set of guidelines for library work distribution.

In 1976, Ed Holley, dean of the School of Library Science at the University of North Carolina, Chapel Hill, said, "Throughout its history the library profession has been plagued with an inability to define precisely what differences exist between the responsibilities of the professional staff and those of other persons who work in libraries."[8] He lamented the controversy that preceded and continued after the adoption of the 1970 "Library Education and Manpower" policy. A generation later, the question of the differences in actual work done by librarians and work done by other staff still required explanation. Ken Haycock observed in 2008 that "the number of professional librarians as a percentage of all staff is declining. More trained paraprofessionals are undertaking work traditionally done by professional librarians."[9] Haycock's statement underscores the contradictions between practices and policies. One has to ask, how could paraprofessionals be doing the work that professional librarians had been doing if that work required a graduate degree? The difference between doing the work and having the job title emerges. According to Haycock, the difference between professionals and nonprofessionals in libraries is that professionals understand the theories and principles on which library work is based, they manage and market libraries, and they train other staff. Haycock cites no studies of work situations, so his portrayal of what happens in the library workplace is not documented. If accurate, it shows a retreat from the requirements for the MLS presented in the

ALA's human resource utilization policy. Like the policy statement, it may be a description of what library educators wish were the situation.

There was no public demand for elaborations in the qualifications of librarians in the 1940s. The push for change came from within the profession. Not only has the public not called for specific qualifications, but most people do not know what the qualifications of librarians are or ought to be, and they are not aware of the distinctions among the employees in libraries. Even a vociferous proponent of using the MLS to define a librarian admitted that "MOST persons popularly known as librarians are not professional librarians."[10] Despite its successes within the library world, the MLS project has had limited success in affecting the status, prestige, or image of librarians in the public mind. As generations of library school students have reported, people are frequently surprised to learn that one can indeed get a graduate degree in library science. A survey of the public conducted for the American Library Association in 2001 showed that "fewer than half (49 percent) thought a college education was required, and only 38 percent were aware that librarians typically hold an advanced degree."[11]

The formal successes of the MLS project have been greater than its public relations successes. Librarians succeeded in codifying the MLS into the definition of librarian in public librarianship by statute or administrative rule, and they succeeded in academic librarianship by achieving recognition in individual campus personnel policies. The way in which this happened varied among types of libraries. Public libraries have been most successful in codifying requirements for librarians. In public librarianship, changes in required qualifications have been written into law or administrative code as a result of lobbying by the profession.

Public librarians have the closest ties to governmental controls over the profession because public libraries are government agencies. At the local level, city and county governments have had to respond to mandates from state library agencies, which have been affected by federal legislation. Federal programs to aid libraries, beginning in the mid 1950s, have been administered through state libraries; to qualify for federal funds, the states have had to develop standards and policies for local library operations, and librarians, who have had a key role in designing these standards, have been able to build the definition of librarian as a person with an MLS into the public library codes, although libraries serving small populations typically are not required to hire MLS graduates. Library associations have used their influence to persuade legislators to enact laws and rules that implement librarians' version of what qualifications should be. There has been little opposition, because it is a matter of little concern to the public and it has been easy for legislators to please library association lobbyists and constituents on this matter. State libraries were the agencies assigned to write service plans and administrative procedures, required for federal aid to states since the Library Services Act was passed in 1957, and these agencies have written a variety of definitions of "librarian," but most recognize the need for an MLS-degreed librarian in all but small library districts. The MLS was not set as a requirement for staff in smaller public libraries because state librarians recognized the practical impossibility of staffing these positions with MLS graduates due to low salaries and remote distances from library schools, complicated by the inability of small towns to compete with the opportunities that cities offer to highly educated people.

For a time, academic librarians were successful in lobbying to have the MLS incorporated into accreditation standards as a required credential for academic librarians, in the standards of such agencies as the Southern Association of Colleges and Schools. Institutional accreditation is required for colleges and universities to have access to federal funding, including student loan programs, so while accreditation has not had the force of law, the standards of the regional accrediting agencies are powerful in shaping academic policies. Specialized accrediting bodies often followed the lead of regional associations in writing their standards. Since the late 1990s, however, the regional standards have shifted focus from higher education institutions' resource commitments and inputs to the learning outcomes of their programs and to assessment of effectiveness in accomplishing institutional goals. The specific requirement for librarians with accredited degrees was an input requirement and has been deleted from most standards for institutional and specialized accreditation. As accreditation standards have changed in the last decade to focus less on inputs (e.g., library staff with MLS degrees) and more on outputs and outcomes, these standards have changed from prescriptions about qualifications of staff to prescripted demonstrations of quality of service.[12]

The MLS degree for library staff is not required by accreditation standards, and it is not a strict requirement for librarian positions in one-third of libraries in the Association of Research Libraries,[13] but it is a required credential for many academic library positions. The Association of College and Research Libraries (ACRL) policy sets the MLS as the required entry credential for librarians and also defines it as the terminal degree in the field, a designation recognized by some institutions in their promotion and tenure policies.[14] The designation of the MLS as both the entry credential and the terminal degree, a somewhat odd situation, results from the desire among some academic librarians to hold the same status as faculty. The ACRL recognized the MLS as the terminal degree in librarianship in 1975 because to have faculty status and advance through faculty ranks, typically the regional institutional accreditation standards require that a person must hold a terminal degree. The ACRL reaffirmed the designation of the MLS as the terminal degree in 2007, even though twenty-four universities offer doctorates in library science.

Whether librarians should or should not have faculty status is a continuing debate among librarians, although it seems to stir little controversy among the professorate or academic administrators in general. Tenure for librarians is confined mostly to smaller colleges and less prestigious universities.[15] The professoriate seems more concerned with the general state of tenure itself and the decline in the portion of teaching faculty who are part of the tenure system.[16]

Success in school librarianship is another story. School librarians, the largest group of librarians, have had a strained relationship with the MLS project. Their concerns have been consistent over a long period. First, they worry about their dual roles as teachers and librarians. School librarians have a long history of prior employment as teachers, and they work in schools where the presence of more than one librarian is rare. School culture privileges teachers over all other school employees except principals. The credentialing process for school librarians is usually layered on top of credentials for teaching, so additional credentials are burdensome. School librarians think of themselves as teachers, and suggestions that they should instead think of themselves as librarians are not well received.[17] Second, the state rules for practicing school librarianship differ from the rules for other kinds of librarians. School librarians and school districts are subject to the various states' certification and licensing rules and do not perceive themselves as subject to ALA rules or policies. Most states do not require a master's degree in library science in order to hold a position as a school librarian.[18] Third, since the 1920s, many school librarian education programs have been housed with teacher education programs in colleges of education as well as in the ALA-accredited master's programs in library schools.

To accommodate librarians in states that do require master's degrees, and in recognition of the needs and educational practices of school librarians, in 1988 the ALA and its American Association of School Librarians (AASL) division began to recognize accreditation of master's degrees by the National Council of Accreditation for Teacher Education (NCATE) as equivalent to accreditation by the ALA for purposes of practicing school librarianship, because many school librarians receive their master's degrees from schools that do not have ALA-accredited master's programs. This accommodation represents recognition of the reality of the situation. Exclusion of thousands of school librarians from the title "librarian" because they do not hold degrees from a school offering degrees accredited directly by the ALA became a politically untenable situation within the ALA and AASL. As explained by the AASL, "For school library media specialists, the appropriate first professional degree is either of the following: A master's degree from a program accredited by ALA, [or] A master's degree with a specialty in school library media from a program recognized by AASL in an educational unit accredited by NCATE."[19] In 2009, thirty-five active programs graduated librarians with NCATE-accredited master's degrees, only five of which also offered master's degrees in programs directly accredited by the ALA.

Academic librarianship has been more successful in requiring librarians to hold an MLS. Here, however, recent changes in the skills required by sophisticated information technologies have led to employment of professionals educated in the computer sciences and technologies, because librarians who come from short MLS programs do not acquire the advanced skills needed. These new academic professionals are hired based on skills and knowledge, not specific credentials. They command salaries equivalent to or greater than librarians' salaries, and they expect professional status. James Neal has referred to them as "feral librarians," a new species of library employees who bring expertise and come expecting professional rewards.[20] This new class of professionals, says Neal, does not share the cultural values of librarians. Whether he is right and how these new professionals relate to library values and academic values and cultures will be revealed in coming years.

Neal's article caused a stir when it appeared in 2006 because a constant in almost all discussions about the professionalism of librarianship has been the importance of an accredited MLS degree. It has stood as an article of faith. The more people who earn it, the more sacred it becomes. However, despite the hopes and despite librarians' fixation on the MLS, the MLS project did not produce the intended outcomes. The MLS was not a magic wand. After the postwar surge, librarians' incomes and status have remained steady. Librarianship has not made important prestige or status gains relative to other professions. The recruits to librarianship are not of greater intellectual skill or accomplishment. The promised enhancements in intellectual sophistication of library science curricula have not been realized, and the desired distinction between professional and nonprofessional work has not been achieved. The gains that professional librarians have made have been largely at the expense of library support staff, whose salary condition has steadily worsened. The MLS is a wedge between librarians, by education and by type of employing library. The cost of library education for new librarians, a cost they mostly bear themselves, is nearly equal to a whole first year of salary. The structure of MLS programs has inhibited development of sophisticated courses with increasingly complex content, particularly in technology, because students enter with no prior knowledge of librarianship except what they may have acquired through employment. The MLS is not only an entry-level degree to the profession, but the courses are also entry level to library science.

TECHNOLOGY IGNORANCE

A major unforeseen consequence of the MLS project is that it rendered library education inadequate in scope to deal with preparing librarians for the information technology revolution. Few anticipated the rapid evolution of computers and network technologies that have so changed the social and economic landscape. In discussions in the 1940s and 1950s, librarians foresaw their future as continuing to be oriented around books, with a few arguing for consideration of audiovisual materials. Computer technologies first changed the way librarians, and others, managed information and materials and more recently began to change the format of information itself from print to digital forms. Library schools were unable to cope with the demands for education about new technologies because the master's program, without prerequisites, made it impossible to provide the necessary sequenced, long programs called for by the nature of computer science, networks, and digital media.[21] Consequently, libraries have been consumers of computer hardware and software products but are not designers of information systems.

Some of the information science programs are longer than the library program, have required knowledge of technology as entrance requirements, and build on an undergraduate base. Information science has become something different from librarianship because of the ability of multilevel, extended curricula to deal with technology. Libraries hire people with degrees in information science or computer science, as described by Neal, to manage information systems that librarians may understand as users but which they do not understand as either engineers or designers. If the expertise of librarians is their knowledge of how to use systems rather than to design systems, does that level of expertise call for graduate training? Does it comprise unique knowledge that qualifies librarianship as a profession?

A CASTE SYSTEM

The MLS project could be seen as merely a disappointment were it not for some of the unintended consequences of the professional policy. An assessment has to ask not only whether a project accomplished its goals but also whether there were other impacts. One of the consequences of the project has been the creation of a caste structure in American libraries, or what Sandy Puccio calls "Jim Crow in our libraries." The economic and status gains of those who have accredited degrees have been accompanied by sharp declines in the status and pay of library technicians. Yet it is not clear that the work itself is different. Puccio says that as a "support staff" person, she did not just do "routine" tasks. "As highfalutin' as we librarians may think we are, support staff is the core of the library."[22] Her message is ambivalent, because while she says support staff are at the core and do important work, she does not want to invalidate the status that the MLS degree gave her, so she says we should look at support staff as "associates in information management or librarians-in-waiting."

Research conducted in conjunction with the Continuum of Library Education Project of the Western Council of State Librarians shows that support staff and library practitioners resent the caste system. They believe they are expected to have, and that they do have, the same competencies that individuals with master's degrees have.[23] In recent years, however, the ALA has engaged in efforts to cement the caste system through the creation of the Allied Professionals Association and through certifications of support status and designation of competencies for support staff that are different from librarian's competencies.

A credentialing process such as the MLS is one strategy for restricting access to an occupation. As described by Kim Weeden, for the group that practices social closure, the strategy "secures advantages at the expense of another group, whether employers or consumers, who must pay a higher price for labor, or other workers, who are denied access to the occupation."[24] The advantages secured may be income, secure employment, status, or other job-related benefits. But library support staff are a principal group at whose expense librarians have made gains.

INCONSISTENCY AND CONFUSION

One of the goals of the MLS project was to bring consistency and predictability to education for librarianship. By standardizing professional education under the rubric of the MLS, library educators would produce graduates whose experiences and skills would be known to employers. From the employer's perspective, the labor market would be predictable and consistent in its expertise. Current critics of library education such as Michael Gorman still preach the need for predictability in graduates, and they have pushed for required instruction in more explicitly stated competencies as the means toward that end.[25]

As Gorman says, there is no assurance of consistency at the moment. Nor is there likely to be, not only because ALA-accredited programs have had so much latitude under the 1992 and 2008 ALA standards but also because there are so many variations in preparation for librarianship. School librarians may be prepared in ALA-accredited programs, in NCATE-accredited programs, in alternative certification programs, or in school library programs in colleges of education that have no specialized accreditation at all. In academic libraries, the need for wide varieties of expertise has led to creation of professional positions that do not call for library education. In public libraries, the variation in preparation and expertise of library workers is greatest. Library technician programs, state library education programs, and college-level education programs are growing in number to meet the need for a skilled public library workforce that only partially comprises MLS librarians. In the absence of bachelor's degree programs that teach basic librarians' skills, community colleges have developed associate degree programs. In 2009, there were fifty-two library technician programs.[26]

The Institute of Museum and Library Services (IMLS) has approved major grants in recent years to enhance alternative training and education for public and school librarians. The ALA has confused the situation by collaborating with the IMLS and with undergraduate library technician programs to develop standards and certification programs for "allied professionals"—library workers who do not meet the ALA's own test for being a librarian (holding an MLS) but whom the ALA recognizes as indispensable "professionals."

The MLS project sought to achieve status for librarians without clarifying their roles except through credentials. The persistent problem is how to define the role of librarians, if it is different from support staff, according to the actual work performed so that librarians can trust that status and prestige will accrue according to what they do, not what degrees they hold. Because librarianship is an organizational profession, the value society places on its services is inextricable from the value society places on libraries as institutions. So long as the institution performs its functions satisfactorily, society at large will be content to let the libraries operate using the staff it can afford, not worrying about internal staffing arrangements.

The fine distinctions among library workers being developed within the ALA will be invisible and of little interest to the various publics whom libraries serve. To library patrons, as has always been the case, the people who work in libraries are all librarians. The distinctions will be noted within the profession, and while they will serve some who will be able to point to certificates on the wall that others do not have, it is doubtful they will serve any purpose from the perspective of library patrons. Library patrons, like the patrons of any profession or institution, expect that libraries, through the librarians who work in them, will provide services that the patrons want. It is possible that the public's expectations will not be honored, or even known. American professions, including librarianship, have developed their work activities and the structures for their work based on their own perception of what is needed. As historian Thomas Bender explains of the "modern service professions," shortly after their formation in the late nineteenth and early twentieth centuries, their "contributions to society began to flow from their own self-definitions rather than from a reciprocal engagement with general public discourse."[27]

Unfortunately, confusion has arisen about what services libraries do provide. The situation was fairly clear in 1950—libraries provided print resources and reference assistance. Book circulation has remained a principal service of libraries. The fairly stable pattern of book circulation over a long period shows some stability in library use, and by inference, some stability in expectations of services. From 1856 to 1978, according to Douglas Galbi, book circulation was steady, at about fifteen books per library user per year. From 1978 to 2004, book circulation declined to fewer than ten books per user per year. Part of that decline Galbi attributes to the aging into adulthood, and lower use of libraries, of the Baby Boom generation.[28] The decline in book circulation in the last quarter-century is but one indicator of a change in the kinds of services that libraries provide and the confusion this has created for librarians and their clients about what purposes libraries serve.

There are some serious mismatches between the professional services librarians want to provide and the kinds of services patrons and sponsors want and expect. School librarians, for example, have sought to redefine their roles within schools without the approval or acceptance of the schools they are supposed to serve. The American Association of School Librarians developed two major initiatives, first through an agenda called "Information Power" that began in 1988 and more recently through a successor agenda called "Learning4Life." The basic concept underlying both projects is that school librarians have a central role to play in school curricula, not as professionals supporting teaching but as professionals who also lead in the schools. The Learning4Life plan says that "AASL works to ensure that all members of the school library media field collaborate with other educators and administrators to provide leadership in the total education program; participate as active partners in the teaching and learning process; connect learners with ideas and information; prepare students for lifelong learning, informed decision-making, a love of reading, and the use of information technologies." The plan continues:

Thus ultimately the goal is to create a shared vision with stakeholders and constituents. Widespread recognition of who we are; our purpose (in 21st-century education); and what students, teachers, administrators, elected officials, parents, and the public can count on school library media programs to deliver is the imperative. And "Learning4Life" is the brand that will symbolize it. . . . [School librarians] will know we have succeeded if school library media specialists recognize and make the connection between the new learning standards and guidelines and content area curriculum standards to improve teaching and learning and impact student achievement; [and] decision-makers value and support the role of the school library media program in facilitating teaching and learning."[29]

The problem for school librarians is that their sponsoring agencies never charged them with such responsibilities and in general have not recognized them as the educational leaders they wish to be. The problems they set out in terms of the concept of information literacy were recognized, but information literacy ultimately became recognized as a broad educational responsibility, not the professional jurisdiction of school librarians.[30] Teachers view librarians' major responsibility as maintaining a collection.[31]

Academic librarians also face a potential mismatch between faculty and student expectations and academic librarians' ambitions. Academic librarians frequently express their desire to be seen as instructional partners, as do school librarians, but as a team of sociologists found, "faculty view librarians as professionals rather than academics and focus more on librarians' service than their educational role." Moreover, said the sociologists, "Librarian-faculty relations have long been a significant component of the profession of librarians. For faculty, however, librarian–faculty relations are of little or no concern."[32] Not only do faculty see librarians as providing a support service, but their reliance on that support is dwindling. Studies conducted in 2003 and 2006 showed that "faculty perceive themselves as becoming decreasingly dependent on the library for their research and teaching needs" and do not view the "consultative role of the librarian" as of the same value that librarians do.[33] Academic librarians seem to be unsure whether libraries are research resources, information commons, virtual entities in some Web-based software, or study halls and social centers—"the library as place." The expertise called for ranges from computer programming to intellectual property law and hospitality management.

Public libraries are confused about their role too, but they have designed a planning process to elicit from their patrons information about what they should be doing. The Public Library Association (PLA) has made positive steps in this regard through the evolution of its planning process. The PLA process features consideration of possible "service responses" which are broad areas in which a library might develop programs. In their planning, librarians are encouraged to start with analysis of community needs and identification of priorities within the possible set of service topics. In this planning approach, library programs are built as responses to community needs, and the public library becomes an instrument that serves the public. The critical question is "What needs to be done?" The latest version of service responses differs from other versions not only in its length (up to eighteen now) but in the way the responses are worded. They are posed not in terms of services the library might provide but in terms of what the library patron might want to be or do, such as be an informed citizen, build successful enterprises, celebrate diversity, or connect to the online world. While PLA's process seeks community participation in selection of services to be offered, the fact that some of these services range far from expected services in libraries shows that there is confusion here too about what libraries should be doing, and thus what skills and expertise librarians should have.

Reliance on the MLS as a credential that in itself establishes professionalism, the heart of the MLS project, is the root of these poor alignments between libraries and their patrons. These mismatches between librarians and their clientele reflect one of the difficulties of "organizational professions," a term Michael Reed uses to distinguish professions composed of managers, administrators, and technicians, like librarians, from the "independent/liberal professions" such as doctors, architects, and lawyers and from "knowledge workers" such as financial consultants or computer analysts.[34] The organizational professions, says Reed, rely on credentialism as a power strategy, using degrees and licenses to control employment and access to positions within bureaucracies. By controlling access to employment through the credentialing processes, organizational professions can perpetuate themselves without first making reference to the needs of their clients; they can say themselves what they perceive client needs to be.

However, like independent professions, organizational professions face competition from the knowledge workers who tend to be entrepreneurial and who use marketing as a strategy for acquiring power.[35] While it may not be time to conclude that independent and organizational professions are in terminal decline, certainly the applications of new technologies suggests the possibility that we are witnessing the twilight of some professions. Librarians actively adopted technologies to replace the functions of library assistants in the last forty years. That most common of activities, checking out books, is now commonly done automatically by patrons themselves, who are familiar with pumping their own gas and checking out their own purchases at grocery stores. Professions that are built on craft skills which they monopolized through credentialism now see their skills duplicated in computer technologies that are accessible through networks that bypass libraries and other bureaucracies.

The clearest example of knowledge workers' challenge to librarianship is the set of Google online search services. Google provides access to many kinds of information through a system that is free, convenient, easy to operate, and effective. Indeed, experiments show that Google is more effective as an information retrieval service than are the systems on which libraries have spent vast amounts of their sponsors' money.[36] Experience with the search systems developed for Internet searches has highlighted users' dissatisfaction with the kind of systems libraries have offered them.[37] Google is doing to libraries what Wal-Mart did to small-town merchants: providing better services at a better price. Small-town merchants reacted to Wal-Mart (and similar firms) by claiming that they themselves embodied their community's values, seeking to preserve their special status and their earnings by appealing to sentiment and nostalgia, often supported by requests for public funds or for restrictions on Wal-Mart's activities.[38] These merchants wanted to keep their place, just as librarians do. But the entrepreneurial knowledge workers have developed products that compete with libraries' services, that do not require the intervention of librarians, and that meet—and through marketing, even create—the information needs of the public. Private-sector entrepreneurs have found ways to make profits on new kinds of information services without charging users. They have, in effect, recreated the broadcast industry of radio and television by providing "free" services whose cost is only the users' attention to advertising. In the Internet age, the key to providing mass access to knowledge and information resources lies not in collecting and cataloging books but in providing free Web access. The contemporary source of democratization of information is the Web, not libraries.

Although it is too early to see comprehensively how libraries will react to the new situation, an early response is not encouraging. Just as small-town merchants responded to change by asking for downtown preservation and renovation funds, librarians are headed to the well to ask for funds to buy software that is designed to replace libraries' online public access catalogs with Google-like systems that will enable users to search at the document level rather than the title level, so that, for example, articles among local library holdings, including licensed materials such as full-text databases, may be located rather than just journal titles.[39] Computer search is not the only example of alternatives to library service models. For two decades now, patrons have been asking that libraries be more like bookstores, and not only because the bookstores are cleaner and sell coffee. The bookseller industry developed a classification system for books that appears to have greater public appeal than the century-old Dewey Decimal System, and recently some public librarians have listened and have done what was once unthinkable, use the Book Industry Standards and Communications system for presenting books to readers.[40] Whether imitation will be a successful strategy remains to be seen. Without the knowledge resources and incentives and openness to competition that characterize entrepreneurial professions, it is not clear that librarianship will be able to do more than to continue to imitate the technology and commercial innovators. If that is the plan adopted, the credentials issue for staff will be a hindrance, as will the approach to services that relies on professional guidance rather than client guidance.

The usefulness of the concept of professionalism to librarianship lies in part in understanding the difference between problems that call for expertise and problems whose resolution depends on values. Many Americans are unwilling to concede that questions of values are questions that call for professional expertise. Rather, they are questions that are left to individuals and groups to resolve based on their ethical principles, religions, philosophies, or cantankerous individualism. That is what it means to be free. The distinction between expertise and values must be carefully maintained. The issues are clear in arenas such as debates about terminal health care and assisted suicides: who is to decide whose life is worth preserving, and for how long? There is a difference between what should be done and how things can be done, and the realms of authority for determining answers in these groups of questions are not the same.

Librarianship sometimes confuses problems of values and problems of expertise. In its strong emphasis on values, the ALA champions positions on issues ranging from constitutional law to U.S. foreign policy or health insurance, but the ALA's justifications for these positions are not founded on professional expertise. Commenting on the political propensities of various professions, Steven Brint argues that the public sector affiliation of some professions is associated with liberalism on social issues. Beyond that, he notes, "moral earnestness is more often evident at the middle and lower levels of the professional stratum. People like to display qualities that bring them credit. For those without the means to make an effective display of wealth and social connections, social credit can be gained by a conspicuous display of moral earnestness."[41] One need not go to library school to be a champion of the First Amendment, nor does graduating from library school make one an expert on what constitutes social justice. In its search for a role, librarianship ought not to forget that libraries are instruments of their sponsors' goals and objectives, not of librarians' goals and objectives. The dangers are many, not least of them being that patron services will be sacrificed to battles between librarians with conflicting values.

One of the most vociferous defenders of democracy, Michael Harris, a longtime critic of the cultural hegemony of libraries, still carries on that tradition when he argues for preservation of libraries as instruments of democratic ideology and in his vision of the democratic aura of libraries as the defining characteristic of librarians' professionalism. Harris would have librarians abandon the illusion of neutrality in promoting values.

But prudence calls for skepticism. Values are important considerations insofar as they relate to professional roles, so that, to begin with, playing the role in a trustworthy fashion is a primary value. In a society where we inevitably have to interact in personal ways with strangers, we must be able to trust that the interaction will be impersonal. That participants will act only on the essential requirements of their roles is of critical importance. As Paul Seabright puts it, "We could not navigate in the bewildering complexity of our social world . . . if we did not have rules of loyalty, of doing as others expect of us."[42] Value statements or positions that are unrelated to the function of a profession are intrusive and violate the implicit client–professional relationship.

Librarians have not consistently approached their profession as an instrument that serves the purposes that patrons and sponsors of libraries have in mind. Librarians' views of professionalism are at the root of that problem.

NOTES

1. American Library Association, Special Presidential Task Force on the Status of Librarians, 2001, www.ala.org.

2. Norman Oder, "Keeping Pace: Budgets Continue Moving Up but Challenges Await," *Library Journal*, January 15, 2007, 55–57.

3. Pierce Butler, *An Introduction to Library Science* (Chicago: University of Chicago Press, 1933), 111–12.

4. Lester Asheim, ed., *Library Manpower Needs and Utilization*, proceedings of the conference cosponsored by the Office for Library Education and the Library Administration Division of the American Library Association with the cooperation of the National Book Committee, March 9–11, 1967, Washington, D.C. (Chicago: American Library Association, 1967), 35.

5. American Library Association, *Library Education and Manpower* (Chicago: American Library Association, 1970).

6. Lester Asheim, "I'm Glad You Asked That," *American Libraries* 2, no. 6 (1971): 597–9, 598.

7. American Library Association, *Policy Manual*, 2007, www.ala.org.

8. Edward G. Holley, "Librarians, 1876–1976," *Library Trends* 25, no. 1(1976): 177–207, 198.

9. Ken Haycock, "Issues and Trends," in *The Portable MLIS: Insights from the Experts*, ed. Ken Haycock and Brook Sheldon (Westport, Conn.: Libraries Unlimited, 2008), 210.

10. Jane Robbins, "Master's Degree from a Program Accredited by the American Library Association Required," a background paper on the value of the master's degree in librarianship commissioned by the American Library Association Office for Library Personnel Resources Advisory Committee, 1987. Typescript copy provided by Nancy Zimmerman.

11. "Public Unaware of Librarians' Education," *American Libraries* 32, no. 5 (2001): 10.

12. Bonnie Gratch-Lindauer, "Comparing the Regional Accreditation Standards: Outcomes Assessment and Other Trends," *Journal of Academic Librarianship* 28, nos. 1–2 (2002): 14–25.

13. Julia C. Blixrud, *The M.L.S. Hiring Requirement: A SPEC Kit* (Washington, D.C.: Association of Research Libraries, 2000), 10.

14. Association of College and Research Libraries, "Statement on the Terminal Professional Degree for Academic Librarians," 1975, www.acrl.org.

15. Rachel Applegate, "Charting Academic Library Staffing: Data from National Surveys," *College and Research Libraries* 68, no. 1 (2007): 59–68.

16. American Association of University Professors, "Contingent Faculty Index, 2007," www.aaup.org.

17. See, for example, the criticism stirred by my essay "Librarian, Teach Thyself" (*School Library Journal* 45, no. 10 [1999]: 45) expressed by Michael B. Eisenberg, "An Open Letter to Dr. Keith Swigger Regarding His Piece in *School Library Journal*, October 1999," *Book Report* 18, no. 4 (2000): 44–45.

18. See Elizabeth A. Kaye, *Requirements for Certification of Teachers, Counselors, Librarians, Administrators for Elementary and Secondary Schools*, 2008–2009 ed. (Chicago: University of Chicago Press, 2008) and previous editions.

19. American Association of School Librarians, "AASL-Recognized Programs Historical List," www.ala.org.

20. James Neal, "Integrating the New Generation of Feral Professionals into the Academic Library," *Library Journal*, February 15, 2006, 42.

21. Susan M. Thompson, "Management and Technology Competencies for the Systems Librarian," in *Core Technology Competencies for Librarians and Library Staff: A LITA Guide*, ed. Susan M. Thompson (New York: Neal-Schuman, 2009), 73–108.

22. Sandy Puccio, "Jim Crow in Our Libraries," *American Libraries* 38, no. 1 (2007): 41.

23. Catherine Helmick and Keith Swigger, "Core Competencies of Library Practitioners," *Public Libraries* 45, no. 2 (2006): 55–76.

24. Kim Weeden, "Why Do Some Occupations Pay More than Others? Social Closure and Earnings Inequality in the United States," *American Journal of Sociology* 108, no. 1 (2002): 55–101, 60.

25. Michael Gorman, "What Ails Library Education," *Journal of Academic Librarianship* 30, no. 2 (2004): 99–101.

26. Council on Library/Media Technicians, "U.S. Library Technician Programs: Includes Certificate, Associate, and Bachelor Degree Programs," 2007, http://colt.ucr.edu.

27. Thomas Bender, *Intellect and Public Life: Essays on the Social History of Academic Intellectuals in the United States* (Baltimore, Md.: Johns Hopkins University Press, 1993), 10.

28. Douglas A. Galbi, *Book Circulation per U.S. Public Library User since 1856*, Social Science Research Network, Working Paper Series, http://ssrn.com.

29. American Association of School Librarians, Standards and Guidelines Implementation Task Force, *Learning4Life, National Plan for Implementation of Stan-

dards for the 21st-Century Learner and Empowering Learners: Guidelines for School Library Media Programs (Chicago: American Association of School Librarians, 2008), www.ala.org.

30. Rhona Oldford, "Teacher-Librarianship and Change: Why Institutionalization Has Failed," *Teacher Librarian* 29, no. 3 (2002): 8.

31. Debra Lau Whelan, "Why Isn't Information Literacy Catching On?" *School Library Journal* 49, no. 9 (2003): 50–53.

32. Lars Christiansen, Mindy Stombler, and Lyn Thaxton, "A Report on Librarian-Faculty Relations from a Sociological Perspective," *Journal of Academic Librarianship* 30, no.2 (2004):116–21.

33. Roger C. Schonfeld and Kevin M. Guthrie, "The Changing Information Services Needs of Faculty," *EDUCAUSE Review* 42, no. 4 (2007): 8–9.

34. Michael I. Reed, "Expert Power and Control in Late Modernity: An Empirical Review and Theoretical Synthesis," *Organization Studies* 17, no. 4 (1996): 573–97, 586.

35. Reed, "Expert Power and Control in Late Modernity," 588–9.

36. Charles Martell, "A Citation Analysis of College and Research Libraries Comparing Yahoo, Google, Google Scholar, and ISI Web of Knowledge with Implications for Promotion and Tenure," *College and Research Libraries* 70, no. 5 (2009): 460–72; William H. Walters, "Google Scholar Search Performance: Comparative Recall and Precision," *Portal: Libraries and the Academy* 9, no. 1 (2009): 5–24.

37. Online Computer Library Center (OCLC), *Online Catalogs: What Users and Librarians Want* (Dublin, Ohio: OCLC, 2009).

38. Jessica Swigger, "Reconstructing Main Street: Memories, Place, and the San Marcos Main Street Program," *Journal of the American Studies Association of Texas* 34 (2003): 35–57.

39. "After Losing Users in Catalogs, Libraries Find Better Search Software," *Chronicle of Higher Education*, October 2, 2009, A13.

40. Barbara Fister, "The Dewey Dilemma," *Library Journal*, October 1, 2009, 22–25.

41. Steven Brint, *In an Age of Experts: The Changing Role of Professionals in Politics and Public Life* (Princeton, N.J.: Princeton University Press, 1994), 207.

42. Paul Seabright, *The Company of Strangers: A Natural History of Economic Life* (Princeton, N.J.: Princeton University Press, 2004), 98.

7

✛

Librarians and
Professionalism

A CONVICTION AND AN AGENDA

The previous chapters discussed the outcomes of the MLS project and suggested some of the reasons for its mixed record of successes and failures. Those reasons include unrealistic ambitions for the MLS vehicle, failures to follow through on academic curricular changes and theoretical challenges, changes in technology, and changes in the social context. Another major explanation for some of the outcomes of the MLS project lies in the concept of professions and professionalization on which the project was founded. This chapter presents a critique of the approach the MLS project took to professionalism and then suggests reconsideration of an older, instrumental model of professions. The question "Is librarianship a profession?" has turned out not to be very useful. In attempting to answer it always in the affirmative, advocates of the MLS project have placed themselves on a Procrustean bed.

In their approach to professionalism, they have confused two issues: whether librarianship is a profession, which is a factual question, and whether it ought to be a profession, which is a question of values. Factual statements are statements about what is, rather than what ought to be. They may or may not be true, depending on the accuracy of the observations of the world on which they are based.[1] Whether it is correct to say that "librarianship is a profession" depends on two things: whether the definition of the category "profession" is accurate and whether the observation of librarianship in terms of that definition is accurate. The definition of "profession" and the characteristics of professions have been topics of discussion, sometimes disputes, among sociologists for a century. As a factual question, determining whether librarianship is a profession has been approached by choosing a definition of the category "profession" and then examining librarianship to see if it meets the criteria for the category. As a values question, whether librarianship ought to be a profession has been approached as a matter of the class and status to which librarians have felt entitled. Values questions can be debated, but the answers given cannot be verified because the answers derive from first principles or assumptions that people make about how things ought to be. The subject of the nature of values and the nature of facts is confusing enough, particularly in the world of postmodern thought, and things really get murky when value statements and factual statements are mixed together in the same argument. And that has often happened in discussions of librarianship and professionalism.

Discussion of the relation between librarianship and professionalism has a long history. In an editorial in *Library Journal* in 1876, Melvil Dewey declared a conviction that has persisted among librarians ever since: "The time has at last come when a librarian may, without assumption, speak of his occupation as a profession."[2] It was important to Dewey, as it has been to subsequent generations of librarians, that librarianship be recognized as a profession because the status of professional has associated social rewards and responsibilities. Status was important to Dewey. His ambitions included desires for personal influence, wealth, and prestige, but they also included ambitions for libraries and librarians.[3] Dewey's 1876 editorial is a statement of a goal asserted, for rhetorical purposes, as it if were a fact. Despite his qualifying phrase "without assumption," Dewey did make some assumptions, and he based his claim for classifying librarianship as a profession on his beliefs about what ought to be true. His argument for classifying librarians as professionals rested on the importance of reading. Individuals who "move and lead the world," he wrote, do so through books. "We shall assume, what few will presume to dispute, that the largest influence over the people is the printed page, and that this influence may be wielded most surely and strongly through our libraries." The library, said Dewey, had come to share with schools the responsibility for "the education of the people." Librarians, no longer mere keepers of books, are the ones who select, organize, evaluate, and recommend books, and librarians teach readers the skills they need so that "they may themselves select their reading wisely." The work of librarians, Dewey argued, is of critical social importance: "there is no work reaching farther in its influence and deserving more honor." Given the importance of books and reading, and the central role of librarians in selecting and guiding reading, he asked if anyone would "deny to the high calling of such a librarianship the title of profession?"[4] The risk of posing a rhetorical question is that some may answer it differently than the rhetorician expects.

When Dewey used the term "professional" in 1876, the word had stronger discriminating power than it does now. "Professions" were those occupations associated with higher learning, leisure, the upper classes, and critical social responsibilities. Dewey's concern was to establish that librarians are professionals and should be accorded recognition and status as such. He did not dwell on the question "What is a professional?" He assumed he and his readers shared elements of the definition of the term. His focus was on showing that librarians are professionals. He appealed to common understandings. The argument that Dewey made for calling librarianship a profession had facets that have become formalized in sociologists' discussions of a trait model of professionalism. A central element of his argument is that librarians have the same traits as other professionals and therefore deserve to be classified with them. In his portrayal of the responsibilities of librarians, Dewey set a pattern for librarians of using the trait model to argue that librarianship is a profession.

THE TRAIT MODEL OF PROFESSIONS

Like Dewey, those who aspire to professional status for their occupational group pose a superficially simple question "Is X a profession?" Early studies of professions took a naturalist approach and posed the logically prior related question, "What are the characteristics in common among the occupations recognized as professions?" In 1933, in one of the first major studies of professions, Carr-Saunders and Wilson focused on studying occupations regarded as professions so that they could infer from them a common set of characteristics, and from which they could inductively construct the category "profession"; they avoided classifying particular occupations as professions and nonprofessions. They did not assume that all professions have all these characteristics either absolutely or to some threshold degree. They concluded from their survey of occupations that "the distinguishing and overruling characteristic [of professions] is the possession of technique. It is the existence of specialized intellectual techniques, acquired as the result of prolonged training, which gives rise to professionalism and accounts for its peculiar features."[5] Carr-Saunders and Wilson concluded that professionals had the following attributes:

- Professionals experience prolonged training to acquire specialized techniques.
- Professionals have direct responsibilities to their clients.
- Professionals use personal judgment in solving problems.

- Professionals form associations to test competence and maintain ethical codes.
- Professionals are self-employed: they charge direct fees to clients for services rather than working in the employ of some other professional person or some business group.

Despite their reluctance to identify particular occupations as professions, Carr-Saunders and Wilson formally established within sociology a "trait model" of librarianship that was already functionally established in the popular educated mind. This is basically the trait model that one finds in Leigh's comments about librarianship as a profession following the Public Library Inquiry.[6] And it is the model on which the MLS project was founded and that has persisted throughout the project's history. Librarians, like those in many other occupations, turned a sociological model into an action agenda. In the agenda derived from the trait model, an occupation can claim to be a profession if it has a set of traits common to occupations that are recognized as professions. The logic of the agenda becomes an extension of the research that led to the trait model: the method for an occupation to become accepted as a profession is to acquire the traits of the recognized professions. In its simplest form, that has been the logic of the MLS project, and it has been embedded in librarianship.[7] It is the model presented in textbooks for library science students.[8]

In 1970, C. Edward Carroll argued that twentieth-century changes in library education, particularly from 1940–1960, "represented the triumph of the professionalizing forces over the counter-forces which had sought to continue the technical training concept of library education."[9] Carroll argued that librarianship had acquired, or soon would acquire, all the defining traits of a profession: "(1) based on a liberal education; (2) requiring a definite period of training offered by special schools; (3) involving a definite body of knowledge rather than mere skill; (4) resulting in practical work rather than solely research or investigation; (5) devoted to service to society rather than to financial gain; (6) concerned with some one human or social need; (7) governed by a code of ethics; (8) usually represented by a national organization; and (9) requiring mental rather than manual labor." Professionalization, Carroll wrote, is "the dynamic process whereby many occupations can be observed to change certain crucial characteristics in the direction of a profession." And professionalism is "an ideology and associated activities that can be found in many and diverse occupational groups where members aspire to professional status."[10] The key words are "ideology" and "status."

There are a number of problems with using the trait model as a simple checklist for professionalization, and they explain some of the difficulties the MLS project has encountered. One problem is that using a model in this way shows a misunderstanding of the purpose of models in social science. Another problem is that the trait model has some limitations: it is static; the trait list may be incomplete; the list may include traits that occupations have but it may overlook traits that they commonly do not have; traits that were unique at one time may become common among many occupations; the social need that occupations address may change or may even disappear.

The trait model is misused when it is understood simply as a tool for deciding whether an occupation is a profession. The analytic power of the trait model is that it guides inquiry by pointing to relevant variables. To understand a particular occupation using a trait model of professionalism, for example, one would look at such features as its professional associations and the nature of its body of knowledge not just in terms of whether the occupation could claim to have those things but in terms of their substance. At the time the MLS project was being formulated, Pierce Butler cautioned librarians to pay attention to the functional traits of professionals, not just to the forms, such as creating and joining associations and issuing certificates and degrees. In 1951, Butler wrote that librarians erred in the attempts to develop a professional identity: "Persuaded of his own professional status, [the librarian] has always been inclined to imitate the outward forms of the other professions before attaining the corresponding internal development." Butler said that librarianship had forms but not professional content. Its major professional association, he said, was "more a labor union than a learned society," and librarianship approached its work "with an empirical rather than a theoretical attitude."[11] Butler went on to argue what the substance of librarianship should be, a social science devoted to understanding the knowledge needs and behaviors of potential library patrons. Whether one agrees that his argument for the proper substance of librarianship is correct, undeniably Butler did use the trait model as an analytic device rather than as a simple classification tool.

Besides the question of appropriate use of the trait model, there are reservations about the model itself. The static nature of the trait model does not account for change, either in the characteristics that define professions nor in the dynamics of those changes. The trait model is an ideal type model developed and embellished early in the twentieth century and most clearly articulated by Eliot Freidson, who says the ideal type "establishes structure, which is fixed and static."[12] The static nature of an ideal type model is part of its analytic strength. However, when models are turned from analytic tools to use in promoting a social agenda, that rigidity becomes problematic both in reasoning and in application. When an ideal type is treated as a recipe rather than as an analytic tool, the implicit assumption is that society at large uses simple logic such as: "Lawyers have degrees; lawyers are professionals; therefore, degrees make professionals." Or "Professionals have graduate degrees; librarians have graduate degrees; therefore, librarians are professionals." If one assumes such a social reasoning, the ideal type becomes a set of orders and an occupational group can set out to make it so. But things aren't so simple. Social reasoning is a soup of logic, implicit and explicit assumptions, opinions, prejudices and preferences, and intermingled concepts.

Another problem of the trait model is that in the analysis of traits of occupations considered professional, the analyst may fail to identify some of the relevant traits. As a result, one might have an incomplete or distorted understanding of what occupations called professions may have in common, and thus might fail to have a complete list of traits. Makers of lists may see some things but may be blind to others. For example, in a world where it is assumed that only males are professionals, it would not be necessary to include gender on the list of traits. In 1950, the vast majority of clergy, lawyers, and physicians were men. Fair or not, occupations that were populated mostly by females, such as teaching, librarianship, and nursing, had difficulty attaining recognition as professions. Similarly, most of the professions generated incomes for their practitioners much higher than the average income for all occupations. Just as in Dewey's time, when professions were associated with upper-income classes, in 1950 professions were associated with high incomes. An incomplete list is a poor compass to use as a guide for development.

The checklist approach also might fail to include in the analysis the traits that occupations recognized as professionals commonly do *not* have. So, even if an occupation acquired all the traits that recognized professions do have in common, an occupation might have traits that none of the recognized professions are perceived to have, and thus the occupation would have difficulty achieving acceptance as a profession. The stereotype of the librarian as a personality may not correspond to items on a list of professional traits, but as perceived by society at large, the set of stereotypical traits of those in the occupation may disqualify the occupation as a profession. One study found that male librarians were stereotyped as "gay, . . . powerless, . . . socially inept, and . . . unambitious,"[13] unlike society's perception of professional men in general. The image of the librarian as a socially inept, unattractive person has persisted for decades. Efforts by librarians to change the image have not been markedly successful, although the greater social sensitivities to stereotyping may have diminished its explicit use.

Another group of traits that might not appear in a model concerns occupations' relationships to institutions and the nature of those institutions. Librarians work in institutions that typically belong to other institutions: public libraries belong to cities or counties (or have public boards that govern them); school libraries belong to school districts; academic libraries belong to colleges and universities; special libraries belong to some host such as a corporation. In the 1930s, Carr-Saunders and Wilson found that recognized professionals tended to be self-employed; they traditionally worked (more or less) autonomously in private practice, for private firms. Most lawyers were independent agents. Physicians did some of their work in hospitals but typically were not hospital employees. Engineers usually worked for private firms. Whether the practitioners of an occupation are entrepreneurs or whether they work only in institutions may affect how society perceives them. From the perspective of librarians, the library is an instrument used in librarians' work,[14] but from the perspective of the lay public, librarians are servants of the institutions that employ them. Librarianship is an institutionalized profession. Whether that association is positive or negative for librarianship as an occupation depends to some extent on how one thinks about libraries.

Thirty years ago, the possibilities for deinstitutionalization afforded by new electronic technologies stirred a continuing debate. Some saw new information technologies as leading to the demise of libraries as institutions. Robert S. Taylor and F. W. Lancaster both argued that libraries would become unnecessary once people could retrieve any text they needed from terminals on their desks, but that the situation provided an opportunity for librarians to divorce their professional identities from these old institutions and their low status.[15] The possibilities in a new world led commentators such as Chung I. Park to suggest that once freed of their ties to libraries, librarians could become "deinstitutionalized information consultants," playing new roles such as "information consultants and producers, information gatekeepers and intermediators, . . . and information equalizers."[16] Looking at the future of libraries, Gregg Sapp documents the ensuing debate within librarianship in an annotated bibliography.[17] For others, the matter of how to regard librarians' workplaces remains contentious because the issues of libraries' roles in the future are ultimately ideological issues, not technological ones.[18]

While the debate may be prolonged, its persistence impacts how the lay public may regard librarians. The lay view of librarians will depend on the nature of the places in which librarians work because the characteristics of the workplace carry over as perceptions of characteristics of the workers. The kind of institution in which an occupation carries out its practice may affect the way the public perceives it, and thus may affect whether it is considered a profession. For example, employment in the public sector is a trait most of the recognized professions in 1950 and thereafter did not have, but the majority of librarians work in the public sector, in schools and public libraries. As Michael Lorenzen says, many libraries, like schools, are publicly owned and often managed by public boards, with substantial citizen input. Lorenzen argues that "the public ultimately controls both schools and libraries and most everyone feels entitled to venture their opinion on how to run them."[19] Eliot Freidson makes the same point when he writes that "in professions that provide personal services to individuals or batches of individuals and whose work is not amenable to detailed formal structuring, organized public forces have greater influence."[20] The cognitive authority of such professions is limited because there is public concern about the social problems with which it deals (censorship and privacy are examples for libraries) and there are many stakeholders who lay legitimate claim to having a voice in the solutions of such problems.

The nature of the workplace affects perceptions of the scope of authority of those who work there. Librarians work in bureaucratic organizations and so are perceived as bureaucrats in contrast to the professions that are mostly practiced independently, such as law and medicine. The power and prestige of bureaucratic professions are linked to the power and prestige of the organization in which they work, and their standing is limited to their work domain. Marie and Gary Radford argue that women librarians are feared within the library setting because they have the power to establish and maintain order there, but they lose their power in the rest of the world because they are women and women in society generally do not inspire fear.[21] One could argue, however, that they are not feared outside the workplace because they are bureaucrats, and in the world outside the bureaucracy, such persons are not feared. Michael Reed says that even within the organization, professionals such as librarians have limited latitude to monopolize and control the knowledge base of their professions. The knowledge of organizational professions, he says, is specific to types of organizations, or even to specific sites, and lacks "the degree of abstract codification and generic application typical of the established professions."[22] Reed says the knowledge held by organizational professions, or bureaucratized professions, is more like the knowledge of a craft than it is like the knowledge of the independent professions.

A further difficulty with the completeness of the trait model is that traits which were unique at one time may not be unique at a later time. Two situations demonstrate the importance of this reservation about the trait model. First, many occupations may claim to be professions. That has long been the case, and in popular usage, "profession" and "occupation" or even "job" are treated as synonyms. Abraham Flexner observed in 1915 that the word "professional" is used loosely, and that "in its broadest significance it is simply the opposite of the word 'amateur,'" the basic distinction being whether one is paid or not for a particular kind of work.[23] Over the decades, more and more occupations used the term, claiming its symbolic value, until in current usage the kinds of traits that led to careful analysis years ago may not be in place now. More important, the term has lost its discriminating value not just through its ordinary use but because in contemporary life, more people now have the traits that were unusual in 1950. By 1950, industrial work had long overtaken agricultural and service work as the primary class of occupations. But for some time now, knowledge work has overtaken industrial work as the primary kind of employment. What was exceptional in 1950 is no longer so. Many occupations now can lay legitimate claim to the traits on the list Carroll used to justify the professionalism of librarianship forty years ago. New work settings have required the spread of education to a significant portion of the population, and mental work is no longer a powerful discriminator. Knowledge work involves technologists who work with their hands and with machines as well as with the knowledge acquired through application of theory.[24] Those who cling to a dated model of professionalism in hopes that it will make them special will find frustration in its application.

Another problem in using the trait model as a checklist is that the social need addressed by an occupation or profession may change substantially. The consequence may be occupational irrelevance. Librarianship's emphasis on its role in reading selection provides a good example. Dewey based much of his argument about the professional nature of librarianship on the unique role librarians played in guiding reading, a role that gave them moral and intellectual authority and responsibilities. In the 1950s, the emphasis on broad general education as a foundation for librarianship was part of the continuation of that thread, of the idea that librarians would guide reading. Two things changed: after Dewey's time there was a new widespread availability of books, and after 1950 there was a general decline in public appreciation for liberal education. Throughout the twentieth century, books became less expensive and more accessible, which meant that it was much more difficult for librarians to guide reading through processes of limited selection. Reading for edification was replaced by enthusiasm for reading as a leisure activity. Books became entertainments. In public libraries, collection emphasis chased rather than guided public taste, and library shelves became filled with best sellers. A broad liberal education was not required to select books based on popularity. And liberal education lost its social position as the purpose of a college education shifted from a particular kind of acculturation to preparation for a career in a specific field. The value of a college education shifted from abstract considerations about personal growth and enlightenment to specific focus on ways to prepare for occupations that paid well. Those who sought to become librarians were not primarily college graduates with broad general educations but older women who had been educated in another major and who, after a time away from school, were becoming librarians as a second career choice. For them, librarianship was a vocation. The kind of broad liberal education that library educators wanted was not realized as a prerequisite to enrollment in library schools in the history of the MLS project.[25]

The trait model presents an ideal type. Ideal types must be understood as heuristics, not exact representations of actual situations; real occupations play out differently in different situations. To understand professionalism in specific times and places, one needs to understand the definition as in the ideal type, but one also has to understand the contexts that shape the particular professions. Freidson calls these contextual variables the "contingencies of professionalism" and states that they "provide the resources for analytic description of how particular occupations in particular times and places come to resemble the model and be called professions or, conversely, lose all resemblance to it."[26]

Freidson says the principal contingencies are the nature of specialized knowledge, the policies and actions of states, and the nature and roles of particular professional associations. To these, one might add other contingencies such as technology and demography, a pair that has impacted the history of librarianship.

American librarians have had mixed success in attracting the support of governments for monopolistic control of library work. Some states have mandated credentials for those employed as librarians, but they have not universally mandated the MLS credential. Librarians have made use of their professional associations to control the profession internally, to some degree, particularly in terms of controlling education for the profession. The ALA, through its published *Standards for Accreditation* and its Committee on Accreditation, has more influence on library education, and thus the preparation of new librarians, than do the library schools collectively. The Association for Library and Information Science Education (ALISE), the association of library educators, has no role in accreditation and no influence over the planning or operations of individual schools. ALISE membership is open to any individuals interested in library education, and library schools hold institutional memberships. The Committee on Accreditation recognizes ALISE as one of the organizations that represent stakeholders in policies concerning library education, but as an organization, ALISE is just one of many stakeholders.

The analysis of "profession" as an ideal type and Freidson's concept of contingencies shed some light on the difficulties of the MLS project in terms of the role and nature of specialized knowledge. Freidson posited three kinds of knowledge: (1) factual and descriptive (scientific knowledge and scholarly knowledge); (2) normative and prescriptive (knowledge of ethics, knowledge of behavior); and (3) esthetic and artistic (knowledge of design, knowledge of criticism). These kinds of knowledge, Freidson says, have different degrees of influence in different historical circumstances.[27] And, one could add, they have different requirements for acquisition. Some of these kinds of knowledge call for extensive formal education in a sequenced program of study, some may be acquired through on-the-job training, and some are not exclusive forms of knowledge at all but are claims upon human conduct that may be based on religious beliefs or personal philosophies and not on unique professional expertise.

The MLS project experienced difficulties in developing a library science, what Freidson calls factual and descriptive knowledge. Hopes that the library school faculties would develop a sophisticated body of knowledge and theory once the programs were at the graduate level were not fulfilled.[28] As Lester Asheim ruefully noted in 1955, "Many of the schools are moving into the fifth year program with little identifiable change in their courses and their requirements."[29] Nor did librarianship develop an esthetic and artistic body of knowledge, or even pose the question "What is beautiful librarianship?" Librarianship rests on principles which are mostly in the category of knowledge that Freidson calls normative. Librarianship has developed standards and guidelines for practices and procedures, but these are not grounded in theory. They guide librarians' behavior in their work, and they also guide librarians' expectations and standards for the ways their clients should behave. Librarians have been particularly active in developing ethical guidelines for themselves and for others, such as the doctrine of intellectual freedom and the adoption of statements of values. The ALA adopted a statement of "Core Values of Librarianship" in 2004. One of the values in that document is professionalism, which is presented simply as appropriate education: "Professionalism: The American Library Association supports the provision of library services by professionally qualified personnel who have been educated in graduate programs within institutions of higher education."[30] Michael Gorman, who played an influential role in writing the Core Values, argues that "ethics and values are the bedrock upon which the work of librarians/information professionals" should be based.[31]

Normative knowledge is not theoretical, however; neither is it tested as science is, nor is it exclusive knowledge. Thus librarianship seems more like law than medicine, in that it is built on policies and conventions and rules rather than on tested scientific theories. Librarianship differs from law, however, in that it lacks the critical support of the state that lawyers have, its associations do not compare to the powerful bar associations that lawyers have, and librarians do not earn the lucrative rewards that lawyers do because the problems librarians deal with are not perceived by their clients to be of comparable critical importance in social interactions. Because the normative knowledge librarianship claims is neither exclusive nor susceptible to proof, it is widely disputed when its implementation affects the values held by others, in matters ranging from the simple—should one be quiet in a library or not?—to the complex, deeply felt matters such as questions pertaining to censorship, selection, privacy, and access to library resources.

POWER AND JURISDICTION MODELS OF PROFESSIONS

The trait model of professionalism was challenged after 1950 by other perspectives. Since then, discussions of the nature of professionalism have involved a dialog among three models of professions. In addition to the trait model, sociologists have presented professions in terms of two other explanatory models: a power model, in which experts are seen to control access to expertise and to benefit from their control by exploiting society's need for their services; and a jurisdiction model, in which professions compete with one another for social recognition of their authority to deal with particular classes of problems.

The Power Model

The power model of professionalism, represented by the work of Magali Larson, presents professionalism as an activity in which professionals gain control over a particular area of expertise, close off access to this expertise, and then sell their services.[32] Larson pointed out that professions are not simply noble service occupations that do good things for society. These occupations are also rewarding to their practitioners who charge for their services. According to Larson, "Professionalization is thus an attempt to translate one order of scarce resources—special knowledge and skills—into another—social and economic rewards."[33] The MLS project was in part an attempt to make knowledge of librarianship scarce by limiting access to it to those who earned MLS degrees. The attempt did not work because the knowledge required to practice librarianship has always been available in other ways, at least as the requisite knowledge is viewed by library clients and sponsors. There are nonaccredited master's programs, state library programs, and most pervasive, skills acquired in practicing the job. The special knowledge of the MLS has not translated into economic rewards in all instances because if no one with an MLS is available, sponsoring institutions have been willing to hire persons trained in other ways rather than to close libraries. The translation of knowledge into economic rewards is the product of a social negotiation that may be conducted implicitly or explicitly. Individual professionals may negotiate their earnings with those who pay them, but librarians are not individual practitioners—they work for institutions, and society (whether through a city council, a school district, a corporation, or a university) considers the cost and value of institutional services in allocating rewards for institutionalized professional services, not the rewards to individuals who work within the institution.

The logic of the power model is that the scarcer the special knowledge, or the more essential clients of professionals perceive it to be, the greater will be the social and economic rewards for providing services that derive from the professionals' specialized knowledge. Educational credentialing, as in the MLS, is one kind of social closure, the restriction of admission to an occupation in order to advance the interests of its practitioners.[34] While closure is often practiced to increase the earnings of practitioners by limiting their supply, that was not the intent of the MLS project, which actually sought to increase the supply of librarians. Librarians have not seen themselves in competition for positions, but rather as in need of more respect and reward for their intrinsic good, not their market position. Librarians have been naive in assuming that their rewards would be associated with their attributes instead of with their market value. They are not alone in this regard. As Weeden says, "Although a given occupation has little control over the cultural value attached to educational credentials, there is no shortage of examples of efforts by emergent or existing occupations to . . . define job requirements and prerequisites in ways that encourage employers to support credentialism."[35]

Where services are not viewed as essential, or as having great value, the rewards for providing the service will be low. And this is the case with librarianship. Society respects libraries, and views them as of cultural value, but whether they are perceived as essential institutions is not clear because surveys conducted by library associations pose questions about the value of libraries without asking respondents to compare the value of libraries to other institutions and services.[36] It also is questionable whether librarians are perceived as providing essential services that could not be provided by educated laypersons or by persons educated in other fields. As Lorenzen says about the low status within universities of library schools and teacher education programs, "the perception in higher education is that librarianship is easy academic work. . . . Most faculty probably imagine they could be librarians if they wanted to be and that their PhD's ought to qualify them for these roles if they wanted them."[37] Librarianship has been unable to secure the market for its services. Weeden explains that in order for an occupation to benefit from controlling access to entry, as librarianship attempts to do through MLS credentialing, the occupation must have some control over the demand for its services, it must be able to direct the demand to its own members, and it must be able to convince consumers that only its members can provide high-quality service. Weeden argues, "If an occupation restricts the supply of workers without also guaranteeing demand for the services it alone can claim, consumers will look for, and other occupations will provide, an alternative source for those services."[38]

The knowledge and skills of professionals are acquired through formal education, which increasingly has become accessible to people of all social classes. In analyzing the means to acquire education called for by professionalism, Larson says that intellectual activity is no longer confined to a class but is found in "a spectrum of classes and enabled by common education."[39] The experience of librarianship suggests that although access to education may be less limited, the rewards of education for an occupation are still arrayed in a spectrum. Equal access to education does not assure equal rewards for being educated.

A "tacit command," in Larson's words, to the professions is that they will develop specialized bodies of knowledge to justify their inclusion in the university ranks. Larson notes that "the most developed and reputable professional schools in medicine, law, and engineering *added* to the prestige of the universities with which they affiliated during the 'academic revolution.' The relationship is inverted in the case of newer professions such as social work, librarianship, and city planning."[40] Indeed, in the era of library school closings, the most prestigious universities, such as Columbia University and the University of Chicago, were among those that jettisoned their library schools. Whether library schools currently add to the prestige of their host universities or are beneficiaries of the universities' status is an open question. About half of the schools with ALA-accredited programs are located in universities that are in the top half of universities as ranked by *US News and World Report*.[41] Thirty-three of the library and information studies schools were assigned ranks in the 2009 report; the rankings of lower-rated schools were not published. Ten of the 33 ranked schools are in universities which are among the top tier (quartile) of universities; 13 are in the second tier; five are in the third tier, and three are in the fourth tier. Two of the ranked schools are in master's degree universities which are ranked among the top 50 institutions in their regions. The status relationship between universities and their schools with ALA-accredited programs is clouded by the fact that 13 of the 15 highest ranked ALA schools consider themselves "iSchools" and are members of the iSchools Caucus.[42] Whether they add to or earn luster from their universities because they are iSchools, not library schools, or vice versa, is unclear, but the high rankings of iSchools as compared to other schools of library and information studies raises a question about whether library schools per se comply with the "tacit command" that Larson observed.

Larson's model is useful in understanding the place of librarianship among other occupations and professions and in society generally. Larson's work is descriptive. It is not a model that provides a prescription for action. However, a research agenda that might derive from it would be to attempt to distinguish the perceived importance of libraries as compared to other institutions, and to assess librarians' perceived value separately from the value of the institutions in which they work. In recent years, the topic of the value-added services delivered by libraries has become popular among librarians, along with discussion of techniques for measuring value as an attempt to garner public support for libraries. An open question is whether demonstrating that libraries are good public or institutional investments, compared to other institutions, would result in more empowered librarians. If inquiries into the value of libraries do not include assessments of the value of librarians, then such works will reveal little about the status of librarians.

The Jurisdiction Model

Beginning in the 1970s, some librarians tried to reframe librarianship in the public mind as "the information profession." The phrase "information society" was becoming widely used, and automation pervaded American work and economic life. Desktop computers were becoming fixtures in offices and homes. Michael Winter voiced an opinion widely shared among librarians when he wrote that the importance of information-related occupations would grow along with increases in the social perception of the value of information as a commodity.[43] Some librarians saw an opportunity here similar to the role Dewey had envisioned relating to reading, but librarians' new domain would include guidance in the use of computer resources in addition to print. The early computer-readable indexes and abstracts and full-text databases were expensive to acquire and difficult to use. Libraries would become the institutions that would provide access to these new tools, and libraries would be gateways to information systems. Librarians would be the professionals who would conduct computer database searches for patrons. Librarians attempted to claim a new niche as "search intermediaries," and discussion flourished about the value librarians could provide as experts who would search databases on behalf of patrons, or at least stand by their sides to guide them through the complexities of new technologies such as telecommunications, search strategies, and search commands, while at the same time introducing them to the importance of librarians' old tools such as thesauri and controlled vocabularies.[44]

Andrew Abbott's *The System of Professions*, published in 1988, became popular among librarians, and Abbott became a prominent speaker at library association meetings, not only because he devoted substantial attention to librarians in his book (other sociological works on professions mentioned librarians only in passing) but also because they saw in Abbott's explanation of the role of professions a rationale for the new role they sought as keepers of information. Abbott defines professions as "exclusive occupational groups applying somewhat abstract knowledge to particular cases."[45] By "exclusive," Abbott means that an occupation has socially recognized authority, or jurisdiction, over a set of problems. That exclusivity, or jurisdiction, is acquired both through the development of expertise relevant to solutions to these problems and through interaction, sometimes competition, with other occupations that have their own jurisdictions. The identification of problems, the development of expertise to address problems, and the processes by which occupational groups become recognized are all elements of what Abbott calls the system of professions.

In Abbott's view, the histories of professions are affected by changes in work itself, by technology, and by "internal intellectual revolutions." The intellectual aspect of professional jurisdiction is critical in his model. As he says, "Abstraction enables survival." Professions develop expertise to address human problems through development of abstract knowledge from which concrete solutions are derived. Professions derive their power from the public's acceptance of the profession's definition of problems and the profession's definition of how a problem should be solved. Abbott argues that in order to be recognized as professions, occupations must have both abstract knowledge and also structures for controlling "the abstractions that generate the practical techniques" for solving problems.[46] Groups that have neither, such as automobile mechanics, are not recognized as professions.

Abbott reveals an academic elitism in this argument, an assumption that ownership and manipulation of theories should be the source of status; that is to say, "people like me deserve high status." Even insightful social scientists can fail to be insightful about themselves. Abbott opens quite a can of worms concerning who owns which abstractions. His argument seems to say that automobile mechanics are not recognized professionals because their solutions to problems are based on knowledge of the material world that derives not from their own work but from the abstractions of physics and chemistry. By that logic, even physicians would not be professionals, because they rely on abstract knowledge created by biologists. And lawyers, whose expertise rests on logic and history, would have difficulty laying claim to any abstractions. In fact, the refusal to ascribe "profession" to many occupations may lie in failure to fully elaborate the subtleties of the trait model. While the trait model overtly identifies some traits, it implicitly rejects others. Mechanics get dirty. Is dirtiness perhaps the essential line for dividing professionals from nonprofessionals? The trait model of professionalism implicitly, and wrongly, assumes that all occupations that require manual labor do not require sophisticated cognitive skills, or that having physical skills is part of some professional roles. Students in library school are sometimes offended when they read position announcements or job descriptions that include a required ability to lift a certain number of pounds of books.[47]

Some librarians concluded from Abbott's jurisdiction model that all they have to do to enhance their professionalism is to compete for new turf. That interpretation of Abbott's argument merely adds one more item to the list of traits a profession must have: it owns turf. In his discussion of these alternative models of professionalism in relation to librarianship, Michael Winter recommended that librarians attempt to develop a composite model that would capture features of each perspective.[48] He maintained that librarianship should be seen in the richer context that was developing in sociological studies of professions. He proposed developing a composite model that would capture features of each perspective, but his suggested models focused on ways to attach the features in those models to librarianship, or vice versa. In effect, he treated the new models as models that added to the list of traits that define professions. Winter's discussion focuses on librarians and their institutions (professional associations and professional schools) and their knowledge base (which he identifies as knowledge of classification and indexing). He does not treat the nature of problems that the knowledge base might solve for clients, nor does he discuss the nature of relations between librarians and clients except to observe that the more librarians are perceived as specialists, and remote from general service to patrons, the more professional they are perceived to be.[49] That line of reasoning was part of a movement, particularly among academic librarians, to put professional librarians in offices, where they could meet privately with clients and where they could work on information products such as path finders and online instruction tools, leaving staffing of public service desks to paraprofessionals and student workers.

Abbott's concept of jurisdiction has been appealing to librarians. However, their hopes for opportunities to enlarge their jurisdiction over information access in the information age were seriously, perhaps permanently, damaged by the rapid pace of continuing developments in the technologies that had given them hope for new powers. Computers became ubiquitous and increasingly easier to operate, and the emergence of the World Wide Web and easily mastered browsers, beginning with Mosaic in 1992, followed by widespread Internet access in homes, schools, and offices, dashed the hopes for professional control over information access. The possibilities for "gateway" and "intermediary" roles seem to be disappearing. With the advent of the Internet, some librarians suggested yet another plan, using the existing library classification and indexing schemes to "catalog" the Internet. But that was also obviated by the inventions of information engineers in other professions who developed a variety of new search algorithms featuring ease of use and automated classification rather than the individual effort of human indexers and catalogers. Librarians' disappointment that they do not play a larger role in information services and in retrieval of information in the Internet age is often accompanied by resentment of the success-ful entrepreneurs who do provide—and shape—society's access to and manipulation of information, while presenting information services in ways that have more popular acceptance than library systems ever did. The new information services enable access to information resources in ways that system users find simple and efficient. The solutions to their immediate information problems call for little expertise because the expertise is built into the system. While users of these systems no doubt recognize the expertise that goes into system design, they do not believe that expertise is required to operate the systems, which is exactly the designers' intention.

Identification of problems is an essential factor in professionalization. If, as Abbott holds, "The tasks of professions are human problems ame-nable to expert service,"[50] then to recognize a profession, the public would have to believe not only that a problem exists but also that its solution calls for expertise, as opposed to readily available knowledge or common sense. Furthermore, society would have to recognize that the expertise called for resides in that profession. This may be the essential problem for librarians.

PROFESSIONALISM AS A SYMBOL

A different explanation of professionalism worthy of attention was pre-sented by the sociologist Howard Becker in 1962. Becker argued that the term "profession" as explained in sociologists' renderings of the trait model was too susceptible to confounding with the popular conception of the term. "Profession," he wrote, "is not the sole property of the social scientist." Rather than attempt to reconcile social scientists' use of the term and laypersons' usage, Becker suggested that the term be treated as an honorific symbol. "We are not concerned with the characteristics of existing occupational organizations themselves but with conventional beliefs as to what those characteristics ought to be. In other words, we want to know what people have in mind when they say an occupation is a profession, or that it is becoming more professional, or that it is not a profession." To make his list of "what people have in mind," Becker reviewed the existing literature on the subject. He then compared the list to the realities of practice of some professions and concluded that the symbolic nature of professionalism made it harmful to society because "the symbol systematically ignores such facts as the failure of professions to monopolize their area of knowledge, the lack of homogeneity within professions, the frequent failure of clients to accept professional judgment, the chronic presence of unethical practitioners as an integrated segment of the professional structure, and the organizational constraints on professional autonomy. A symbol which ignores so many important features of occupational life cannot provide an adequate guide for professional activity." He went on to say, "Professional education tends to build curricula and programs in ways suggested by the symbol and so fails to prepare its students for the world they will have to work in," adding in a footnote, "It is my impression that those schools that pay most attention to the realities of the work are apt to be labeled with the invidious term 'trade school.'"[51] Becker's indictment of professional schools could apply to the approach taken by library schools in the MLS project as they claimed to segregate "the realities of work" into training for nonprofessionals while reserving to the MLS programs education in the ethics and prerogatives of professionals.

Librarianship was not the only occupation that sought to enhance its status by adopting more trappings of professionalism in the 1950s. What these occupations really sought was to associate themselves with professionalism as a symbol. In the 1950s, librarians, nurses, optometrists, and social workers were among those who sought to enhance their standing. As Becker argued, "they attempt to appropriate the symbol by taking on as many of its features as practical. They subsidize research, they adopt codes of ethics, they lengthen the period of required training, and so on."[52] The similarities among these occupations' approaches are striking. A 1957 article by Ernest Greenwood about his occupation, social work, reads just like articles about librarianship; substitute "librarian" for "social worker" and his essay becomes like many works on librarianship at the time.[53]

The occupations seeking to affiliate themselves with professionalism as a symbol seem not to have realized that while one can traffic in symbols, one cannot control their use or meaning. The trappings of professionalism are inconsequential if there is little demand for an occupation's services. One of the tasks assumed by professional associations such as the ALA has been to enhance demand for library services and to channel the demand to professional librarians. This has been attempted through market slogans such as "Ask a Librarian" and promotions such as National Library Week. However, Weeden found that associations' impact is insignificant in enhancing occupations' rewards: "Apart from their licensing and certification activities, occupational associations have virtually no control over the labor supply and must rely on largely symbolic claims to

protect task jurisdictions. Association rhetoric resounds with such symbolic claims, but apparently no one is listening."[54]

In the same period when many occupations aspired to professionalism,
professionalism came under attack as elitist, exploitative, and undemo-
cratic, in the work of Larson and in such books as Jethro Lieberman's *The
Tyranny of the Experts*.[55] Attacked directly from some quarters, professionalism also evolved in response to changes in technology, in information
dissemination, in business practices, in capital accumulation, and toward
globalization, so that the exclusive control of knowledge capital that was
at the heart of professionalism became restructured.[56] Whether librarianship, or one of the other aspirant occupations, is considered a profession
may be a less important question now than it was fifty years ago, because
now so many occupations claim to be professions and the term has lost
much of its discriminating power. Recognition of professional status is
not as strong as it once was as a determinant of occupational rewards.

A FLAWED CONSTRUCT

The concept of professionalism in the MLS project was flawed because
it focused on the characteristics and rewards of librarians rather than on
the needs of clients or on the kinds of expertise required to serve them.
The concept served neither librarians nor their clients because it focused
on the status of librarians rather than on their functional roles. Librarians
who created the MLS project did not have a useful understanding of the
nature of professionalism. They made a flawed model the foundation of
the MLS project in part because they were misled by a simplistic use of
the trait model and in part because they did not recognize the limitations
of that model. In the MLS project, librarians assumed that if they pursued
the traits on the ideal type checklist, society would respond with recognition of their worth. That showed a naive understanding of professionalism. The models of professionalism introduced by sociologists enrich understanding of librarianship and other occupations by providing frames
for comparing and contrasting groups according to new sets of variables.
Each explains some aspect of librarianship's modest successes as a profession and sheds light on its failure to achieve all its aspirations. Librarianship has not controlled exclusive expertise and knowledge resources
that meet the substantive requirements of the trait model and which are
perceived as critically important, and it has not had clear and exclusive
responsibilities for problems the public recognizes as vitally important.
While these models show that the goal of achieving status and recognition calls for a strategy much more sophisticated than a simple checklist,
neither the power model nor the jurisdiction model serves librarians any

better as blueprints. Bonnie Nelson may have been right when she wrote that "trying to meet the attributes of a profession as laid down by sociologists is a waste of time and energy," but she went too far in saying in the same sentence that "professionalism is a false goal."[57]

Professionalism is not a false goal, but it must be pursued pragmatically, and the meaning of the term must be understood functionally. Professionalism is best seen as a relationship, not a trait. Whether one calls the relationship a power relation or a responsibility relation, like all relationships it involves some sort of commitment by the parties involved. Relationships of any kind are built on mutually recognized interests, agendas, or problems. Professionals play one role, and clients play another. Their complementary roles are linked not by their mutual status but by the fact that one has a need and the other may have a solution that is based on training and tested standards for practice. Successful relationships involve negotiation and interaction. Librarianship adopted the MLS project to address some of its own problems and its ambitions for higher status, but these were not recognized as important problems by librarians' clients. They were not problems associated directly with library service as patrons perceived it, so the project had no functional importance to library patrons. There was no public call for librarians to acquire master's degrees, nor was an argument made that focused on possible improvements to library service as a result of the graduate degree requirement. The MLS project was not rejected by the public; it was simply ignored, because it was never presented to them.

A PROFESSIONAL RESPONSE TO CONSIDER

While this is not the place to develop a new model for librarianship in the context of professionalism, it would be unseemly to criticize one approach without suggesting at least some aspects of an alternative. The relationships between occupations and the larger society are not simple, and achieving the opportunities, status, and rewards of professionalism is not an autonomous process of putting on the right suit or acquiring degrees. Rather, it is the result of interactions in which occupational groups earn recognition by solving clients' problems as seen by the clients through the services they provide, the controls they are able to apply, and the value their work is perceived to have. If the approach to professionalism embodied in the MLS project did not lead to a satisfactory outcome, what different strategies might librarians consider?

Librarians would do well to recall the 1947 National Opinion Research Center survey about professionalism to see again the emphasis people have always placed on the importance of the work to be done, not the importance of the workers who do it.[58] It also would be useful to remember Pierce Butler's call, in 1933, for a library science based on a study of community needs: "A professional library worker must possess a scientific, generalized knowledge which will enable him to discover the complex library needs of a mixed community."[59] Butler's direction to professional librarians demands that they understand what communities need and what libraries can offer, and then match their knowledge to these needs. His charge is reminiscent of Plato's approach to occupations in *The Republic*, where Socrates and his friends discuss the creation of a just state. As an intellectual exercise, they ask what a just society would be like if it could be invented, without a history. In commenting on the institutions the state would require, Socrates says that necessity is the mother of invention.[60] Societies make institutions and create agencies as they need them. Although few societies are created from scratch according to some design (there are exceptions to be seen in some utopian communities), it seems clear that social agencies come and go as society finds them more or less useful. Socrates' approach suggests that we think of occupations as functional instruments or agents created by society to accomplish essential tasks. The essential nature of these agents is service to society, not the occupations' areas of jurisdiction or the power that might accrue to them. The traits the occupations' members have are those that are necessary to the work the occupations perform.

One of the misunderstandings of professionalism is the conception that there is one single model for describing all professions. Freidson and other sociologists have shown that there are different kinds of professions and they must be understood differently, depending on what Freidson calls their "contingencies," that is, the ways they interact with their social environments and the kinds of knowledge bases from which they operate.[61] The professions may all be seen as instruments, but they are not all the same kind of instrument. There is no need to abandon the concept of professionalism because librarianship does not fit one of the models, or more properly, vice versa. The concept is valuable if what we look for is what underlies all the models, and that is not a body of knowledge but the fact that from the perspective of clients, all professions are instruments for solving problems. If the term "instrument" or "agency" seems too abstract, perhaps the term "problem solver" would be clearer, because that is what professions are from the client perspective. Different problems call for different solvers. For the craft professions like librarianship, the set of solutions available includes professional expertise.

A useful way to think about professionalism is to regard professions as services or agents who handle society's needs through the exercise of expertise. In light of the complex renderings of professionalism in the sociology literature, that statement may seem too simple, but what is most needed in all this discussion is clarity. While librarians have been vocal in their desire to be seen as professionals, they have not been clear about either the problems librarianship addresses nor about the nature of the expertise they apply to those problems. The original problem American librarianship addressed was easy to grasp: how to share scarce books with many readers. The problem became more complex as both the population and the number of published books grew, and consequently as libraries grew in scale, leading to problems of book selection and book description. Those problems then became enlarged and somewhat confused as the discussion shifted to "documents" and "documentation," and then became amorphous when the problem became "information access." A question to ponder is whether the problem of providing shared access to materials that are too expensive (in cost, space, storage, etc.) for individuals to acquire on their own remains an important social need to be addressed by the institution of the library.

What other social problems librarianship should handle now and in the future is the subject of much debate within librarianship in its literature, at conferences, and in the various electronic discussions.[62] In considering the various proposals, one always has to return to fundamental questions: Are there social problems that call for expertise and is that expertise available in librarianship? Or is librarianship a body of expertise looking for a problem to solve? The key to professionalism lies in the nature of problems to be addressed. If the role of professions is to address problems that call for expertise, then when those problems no longer exist, or when their solutions no longer require expertise, or when the expertise of a particular profession is no longer relevant to current problems, then there is no role left for that profession. On the other hand, problems may become more complex and may demand that the profession which is society's agent for working on such problems extend its professional knowledge, the technological sophistication of its instruments, and the depth and length of training and education of those who practice the profession. Analysis of the work to be done and the foundations on which it rests could lead to a different understanding of the professional education needed.

The question "Is librarianship a profession?" is unproductive. A more important question is "What are the functions of libraries as social instruments?" That is not a question for librarians to answer alone or in a self-serving way. Straightforward answers unclouded by vision statements and ideological jargon will enable clear thought about the work librarians do and how they should be educated to do it. Until librarians can answer the question of function without rhetorical flourishes, more complex questions and answers will perplex them.

NOTES

1. Herbert A. Simon, *Administrative Behavior: A Study of Decision-Making Processes in Administrative Organizations*, 4th ed. (New York: Free Press, 1997), 56.

2. Melvil Dewey, "The Profession," *American Library Journal*, September 30, 1876, 5–6.

3. Wayne A. Wiegand, *Irrepressible Reformer: A Biography of Melvil Dewey* (Chicago: American Library Association, 1996).

4. Dewey, "The Profession," 5–6.

5. A. M. Carr-Saunders and P. A. Wilson, *The Professions* (Oxford: Oxford University Press, 1933), 284–7.

6. Robert D. Leigh, *The Public Library in the United States: The General Report of the Public Library Inquiry* (New York: Columbia University Press, 1950).

7. Dale Eugene Shaffer, *The Maturity of Librarianship as a Profession* (Metuchen, N.J.: Scarecrow, 1968), 18–19.

8. For examples, see Jean Key Gates, *Introduction to Librarianship* (New York: McGraw-Hill, 1968); and Richard E. Rubin, *Foundations of Library and Information Science*, 2nd ed. (New York: Neal-Schuman, 2004). Rubin nods briefly to other models, but his emphasis is on the trait model.

9. C. Edward Carroll, *The Professionalization of Education for Librarianship, with Special Reference to the Years 1940–1960* (Metuchen, N.J.: Scarecrow, 1970), 248.

10. Carroll, *The Professionalization of Education for Librarianship*, 29–30.

11. Pierce Butler, "Librarianship as a Profession," *Library Quarterly* 21, no. 4 (1951): 235–47, 237, 245.

12. Eliot Freidson, *Professionalism: The Third Logic* (Chicago: University of Chicago Press, 2001), 7.

13. Aloha Record and Ravonne Green, "Examining Gender Issues and Trends in Library Management from the Male Perspective," *Library Administration and Management* 22, no. 4 (2008): 193–8, 197.

14. Ralph A. Beals, "Education for Librarianship," *Library Quarterly* 7, no. 4 (1947): 296–305, 297.

15. Robert S. Taylor, "Reminiscing about the Future: Professional Education and the Information Environment," *Library Journal*, September 15, 1979, 1871–5; Frederick Wilfrid Lancaster, "Whither Libraries? Or, Wither Libraries?" *College and Research Libraries* 39, no. 5 (1978): 345–57.

16. Chung I. Park, "Transforming Librarians," *COINT Reports* 5, no. 5 (1984), Eric Document ED257469.

17. Gregg Sapp, *A Brief History of the Future of Libraries: An Annotated Bibliography* (Lanham, Md.: Scarecrow, 2002).

18. Michael H. Harris, Stand A. Hannah, and Pamela C. Harris, *Into the Future: The Foundations of Library and Information Services in the Post-Industrial Era*, 2nd ed. (Greenwich, Conn.: Ablex, 1998).

19. Michael Lorenzen, "Education Schools and Library Schools: A Comparison of Their Perceptions by Academia," *Illinois Libraries* 82, no. 3 (2000): 154–9.

20. Eliot S. Freidson, *Professional Powers: A Study of the Institutionalization of Formal Knowledge* (Chicago: University of Chicago Press, 1986), 223.

21. Marie L. Radford and Gary P. Radford, "Power, Knowledge, and Fear: Feminism, Foucault, and the Stereotype of the Female Librarian," *Library Quarterly* 67, no. 3 (1997): 250–66.

22. Michael I. Reed, "Expert Power and Control in Late Modernity: An Empirical Review and Theoretical Synthesis," *Organization Studies* 17, no. 4 (1996): 573–97, 584.

23. Abraham Flexner, "Is Social Work a Profession?" *School and Society*, June 26, 1915, 901–11, 901.

24. Peter Drucker, "The Age of Transformation," *Atlantic Monthly*, November 1994, 53–80, 56.

25. Butler, "Librarianship as a Profession"; Beals, "Education for Librarianship."

26. Freidson, *Professionalism*, 7.

27. Freidson, *Professionalism*, 157–9.

28. See Sydney J. Pierce, "Dead Germans and the Theory of Librarianship," *American Libraries*, 23, no. 8 (1992): 641–3. Pierce set off a discussion that continues to the present about what constitutes the theoretical base of librarianship. See, for example, John Buschman, "The Integrity and Obstinacy of Intellectual Creations: Jurgen Habermas and Librarianship's Theoretical Literature," *Library Quarterly* 76, no. 3 (2006): 270–99.

29. Lester Asheim, "Education for Librarianship," *Library Quarterly* 25, no. 1 (1955): 76–90, 83.

30. American Library Association, "Core Values of Librarianship," www.ala.org.

31. Michael Gorman, "Professional Ethics and Values in a Changing World," in *The Portable MLIS: Insights from the Experts*, ed. Ken Haycock and Brook Sheldon (Westport, Conn.: Libraries Unlimited, 2008), 15.

32. Rubin, *Foundations of Library and Information Science*, refers to this model as a control model; in his textbook for librarians he argues that what librarians control is a body of skills that they use for the public good; thus they are oriented toward service, which is one of the features of the trait model. In effect, he turns the control model on its head and says librarians are best understood as professionals in terms of having the trait of service, which is what they control.

33. M. S. Larson, *The Rise of Professionalism: A Sociological Analysis* (Berkeley: University of California Press, 1977), xvii.

34. Kim A. Weeden, "Why Do Some Occupations Pay More than Others? Social Closure and Earnings Inequality in the United States," *American Journal of Sociology* 108, no. 1 (2002): 55–101, 58, 59.

35. Weeden, "Why Do Some Occupations Pay More than Others," 62.

36. Texas Library Association, *TLA Texas Voter Survey on Libraries*, 2008, www.txla.org; OCLC, *From Awareness to Funding: A Study of Library Support in America* (Columbus, Ohio: OCLC, 2008).

37. Lorenzen, "Education Schools and Library Schools."

38. Kim Weeden, "Why Do Some Occupations Pay More than Others?" 66.

39. Larson, *The Rise of Professionalism*, xiv.

40. Larson, *The Rise of Professionalism*, 201.

41. "Best Colleges 2010," *U.S. News and World Report*, September 14, 2009, http://colleges.usnews.rankingsandreviews.com/best-colleges.

42. The iSchools Caucus, www.ischools.org.

43. Michael F. Winter, *The Professionalization of Librarianship*, University of Illinois Occasional Papers 160 (Champaign, Ill.: Graduate School of Library and Information Science, University of Illinois, 1983).

44. See, for example, Bruce D. Bonta, "Online Searching in the Reference Room," *Library Trends* 31, no. 3 (1983): 495–510; Mary M. Hammer, "Search Analysts as Successful Reference Librarians," *Behavioral and Social Sciences Librarian* 2, nos. 2–3 (1982): 21–29; Joseph E. Straw, "From Magicians to Teachers: The Development of Electronic Reference in Libraries: 1930–2000," *Reference Librarian* 74 (2001): 1–12.

45. Andrew Abbott, *The System of Professions: An Essay on the Division of Expert Labor* (Chicago: University of Chicago Press, 1998), 8.

46. Abbott, *The System of Professions*, 246, 30, 8.

47. For discussion of the knowledge required for some kinds of manual work, see Mike Rose, *The Mind at Work: Valuing the Intelligence of the American Worker* (New York: Penguin, 2005); and Matthew B. Crawford, *Shop Class as Soulcraft: An Inquiry into the Value of Work* (New York: Penguin, 2009).

48. Winter, *The Professionalization of Librarianship*, 37–41.

49. Michael F. Winter, *The Culture and Control of Expertise: Toward a Sociological Understanding of Librarianship*, Contributions in Librarianship and Information Science 61 (New York: Greenwood, 1988), 65–66.

50. Abbott, *The System of Professions*, 35.

51. Howard S. Becker, "The Nature of a Profession," in *Sociological Work: Method and Substance* (Chicago: Aldine, 1970), 87–104; the essay first appeared in *Education for the Professions*, 61st Yearbook of the National Society for the Study of Education, part 2 (Chicago: University of Chicago Press, 1962), 27–46, 90, 93, 103.

52. Becker, "The Nature of a Profession," 97.

53. Ernest Greenwood, "Attributes of a Profession," *Social Work* 2 (July 1957): 45–55.

54. Kim A. Weeden, "Why Do Some Occupations Pay More than Others?" 83.

55. Jethro K. Lieberman, *The Tyranny of the Experts: How Professionals Are Closing the Open Society* (New York: Walker, 1970).

56. Michael I. Reed, "Expert Power and Control in Late Modernity: An Empirical Review and Theoretical Synthesis," *Organization Studies* 17, no. 4 (1996): 573–97.

57. Bonnie R. Nelson, "The Chimera of Professionalism," *Library Journal*, October 1, 1980, 2029–33.

58. NORC, "Occupational Prestige Studies/Summary," http://cloud9.norc.uchicago.edu/faqs/prestige.htm.

59. Pierce Butler, *An Introduction to Library Science* (Chicago: University of Chicago Press, 1933), 111.

60. Plato, *The Republic*, translated by B. Jowett (New York: Vintage, 1965), book 2.

61. Freidson, *Professionalism*.

62. For examples, see Rae A. Earnshaw and John A. Vince, *Digital Convergence: Libraries of the Future* (New York: Springer, 2007); John E. Buschman, *Dismantling the Public Sphere: Situating and Sustaining Librarianship in the Age of the New Public Philosophy* (Westport, Conn.: Libraries Unlimited, 2003); Jeannette Woodward, *Creating the Customer-Driven Academic Library* (Chicago: American Library Association, 2009).

8

✝

What Could Be Done?

Between 1880 and 1900, the American professional, as analyzed by Samuel Haber, "asserted that he was neither a capitalist nor a worker, rather that he stood in some third position with an outlook arising from [scientific knowledge]."[1] For librarians, the conviction of their professionalism, however, was not that they believed they had developed a scientific knowledge of librarianship. Rather, their belief that they belonged among the ranks of professionals stemmed from their belief that their work was professional because they dealt with selection, collection, and access to the physical containers of intellectual work. Dewey, who gets praised and blamed for much that has happened in American librarianship, was the leading proponent of the argument that librarians' value derived from their association with books. Books were the physical embodiments of intellectual values at the end of the nineteenth century, the time when, according to Haber, professional work came to be recognized as "largely intellectual." Librarians have been quick to associate their value with the value of the knowledge records for which they are responsible, or with the ideological principles of free libraries, as if the aura of libraries as emblems of culture or social justice would transfer to an aura for librarians. Librarianship has suffered at the hands of its celebrators. Louis Shores, a longtime library educator, often referred to librarianship as "an occupation of destiny."[2] It was a ringing phrase, but if librarianship has a destiny, so does every other occupation. Despite its respect for libraries as institutions, society has not seen librarians in the positive ways in which they see themselves. Consequently, librarians often feel unappreciated and sometimes even resentful. They set themselves up for disappointment.

Dewey's declaration asserted a conviction and set an agenda in which librarians have persisted for 130 years. Librarians thought the adoption of the MLS project was a big step toward accomplishing their goal of acceptance as a profession. Although there were some who demurred after the difficult employment period and the library school closings in the 1970s, arguing that the quest for professionalism was contrary to librarians' own economic self-interest and to the needs of their clients, these voices were isolated and were not heeded.[3] The conviction that librarianship is a profession has provided inspiration and pride among librarians, but it also has been problematic for them because the expectations it encourages are often contradicted by librarians' experiences.

Sociological models are heuristic devices. They are valuable insofar as they teach useful lessons or initiate threads for research. Professionalism is not a natural category into which occupational species do or do not fall neatly. Whether explained as a trait model, a power model, a jurisdictional model, or a symbolic category, it is a social construct, so it is what it is for each culture or subculture. To frame the point in a system suggested by George Kelly, each person has his or her own personal construct or theory about how some segment of the world works; people in groups may share a construct.[4] The MLS project is a construct about the relation between social rewards and professional education. Constructs, says Kelly, are like scientific hypotheses: they are the bases for predictions about what courses of action are likely to be successful. Each action is like an experiment in that it is a test of the construct. If the construct leads to action that is repeatedly unsuccessful, the reasonable thing to do is to reject the construct and replace it with another model of reality. Persistence in a model that is inconsistent with the facts is bad science. When a theory does not stand up to testing—that is, it fails to predict outcomes of actions—then the reasonable person or group abandons the theory.

Evidence shows that the MLS project has been costly, has created confusion outside librarianship and polarization within, and has accomplished some but not all of its objectives. The same complaints from librarians about recognition are made decade after decade, and the same issues concerning who should do what kinds of work in libraries and concerning the nature of library education are argued repeatedly. It is unhealthy to persist in adhering to a model that time after time fails to produce the outcomes one wants. Furthermore, many of the conditions that led to adoption of the MLS project no longer exist. It is time to consider some different models.

For decades, there has been much discussion about what is or is not wrong with library education. That discussion has taken place within librarianship, which is a relatively small community. The ALA reports that there are 134,355 employed librarians in the United States, fewer than the number of people who attend a single NASCAR race at Texas Motor Speedway or Daytona. In addition to the librarians, there are 195,586 other paid staff.[5] No one outside librarianship pays much attention to library education or librarians' credentials. The community of library sponsors and library patrons is concerned with the availability and quality of services, not with the credentials of the people who deliver the services. In the jargon of assessment, those served by libraries are interested in outcomes, not inputs.

The absence of strong outside interest in the education of librarians is good for librarians insofar as it simplifies a process; there is unlikely to be much interference with what librarians decide, whether it is to make changes or to retain the current system. That absence of interest is bad for librarians, and their public, because it means that just as in the case of the MLS project's beginnings, there will be little involvement of the primary stakeholders in the decision and planning processes. If the interests of library patrons and sponsors are to be served, and if ideas they might have are to be heard, it will be up to the library community to take proactive steps to discover the views and interests of those whom libraries serve concerning what changes may be called for. Selden says that accrediting is contention for control over standards.[6] In such a debate, who speaks for the library patrons' interests, and who speaks for the interests of present and potential students who seek to become librarians?

What might be useful at this point is to examine the options concerning preparation of new professionals. What follows is a discussion of the alternatives offered, the principles and evidence associated with each, and their advantages and disadvantages. There are four major options for library education: continuation of the present system; separation of library education from information science education through creation of new accrediting agencies for master's degrees in information science; recognition of bachelor's degrees, either in lieu of or in addition to accreditation of master's degrees; development of multiple models for professional training.

CONTINUATION OF THE PRESENT SYSTEM

The principle underlying continuation of the present system is the same as it was in 1950, the belief that higher levels of education will confer status and prestige on the profession. The goals of the MLS project have been repeated so many times that instead of serving as goals, they now serve as unexamined principles. The main advantage of continuing the present system is that it requires the least thought and organizational effort. The ongoing squabbles have become comfortable. Those who are interested can continue to debate the merits and scope of library science and information science, the proper content of lists of competencies, the procedural issues of which groups were or were not consulted and when. All can be united in two main lamentations: that persistence in the same course of action does not lead to new outcomes, and that the only problem is that Others fail to understand Us. The main disadvantage of continuing the present system, in addition to the concrete outcomes described in previous chapters, is that there is no reason to expect different outcomes as long as one keeps on doing the same things.

In the present system, library education programs submit to a review by the ALA Committee on Accreditation (COA) every seven years, or every three if they are conditionally accredited. There is no discernible sentiment for change among the library schools, even though the accrediting process is time-consuming and costly, and schools worry about receiving an unfavorable review because that could impact their enrollments and their standing within their own institutions. Library education is a small world, and the decisions made by the COA about schools are widely known. Schools that receive conditional accreditation do not do well in peer reviews and published rankings of schools. However, it is rare that a school actually loses accreditation.

Discussions about the existing system seldom question the basic concept of the system or the processes of accrediting. Rather, they focus on occasional modification of the standards. Modifications are rare and are accomplished only after long deliberation. Any change process moves slowly, impeded by COA practices that assure no radical moves. Even getting proposed changes on the table takes years, and after a proposal is made, there is an extended period of review. The review of the ALA's 1992 *Standards for Accreditation* took five years, from 2003 to 2008. Accrediting is a serious and expensive process, and if changes are sudden and frequent, the goal of predictability, which is fundamental in creating accreditation in the first place, will be in jeopardy. A recent example of attempts to change library education occurred in spring 2009, after the ALA Council's adoption in January 2009 of the recommendations of the Presidential Task Force on Library Education, which had been appointed in 2006 by then ALA president Leslie Burger. The COA sent a letter to the Council in June 2009 explaining the need for a deliberative approach and setting a calendar for reflection and review with the possibility of presenting an action item to the Council in January 2013.[7] The COA makes recommendations to the governing body of the ALA, the ALA Council, concerning accreditation standards. The COA makes its accrediting decisions concerning specific programs independently, but in other matters, the COA is an agency of the ALA and is under ALA control.

While continuation of the present system will not result in sudden changes in standards, a consequence of continuation may be that other approaches to library education and to hiring practices will go on without direct attention from the COA or ALA. In effect, the COA closes its eyes to developments in the world outside the realm of the accredited MLS. While the present system continues, evolving at a glacial pace, other changes may happen independently of the ALA and COA.

CREATION OF NEW ACCREDITING AGENCIES FOR MASTER'S DEGREES IN INFORMATION SCIENCE

The principle for distinguishing between information science (IS) and library science (LS) programs, and confirming that distinction through separate accreditations, is that IS and LS are different intellectual and professional endeavors. The advantages of separation are that each would have a sharper focus for the expertise of its graduates. The disadvantages are cost and uncertainty about whether IS programs are positioned strategically or sufficiently understood to survive without the legitimacy and enrollment provided by affiliation with library education. Despite the ongoing squabble about the differences, the programs are still interdependent at least organizationally.

One of the recommendations of the Presidential Task Force on Library Education in 2009 was that in order to be accredited, a majority of full-time faculty of programs must be "grounded in librarianship, by virtue of their educational background, professional experience, and/or record of research and publication."[8] The recommendation was a response to discomfort among many librarians about the confusion between library education and information science education. The way accrediting works in librarianship contributes to the confusion. As their degrees came up for renewal of accreditation under the 1992 *Standards*, some library schools presented their information science degrees for ALA accreditation. They were able to do that because the 1992 *Standards* emphasized institutional goals and processes, not program content. The 1992 *Standards* adopted the deliberately ambiguous phrase "library and information studies" as the name for the field. Confusion followed.

An outcome of the 1999 Congress on Professional Education was the creation by the ALA Executive Board of the Task Force on External Accreditation and Scope of Accreditation, whose charge was "to explore the possibility of an independent board for accreditation and to determine whether ALA is accrediting programs for librarians only or also for other information professionals."[9] The task force drafted a report recommending a separation between library science and information science accreditation, but the deans and directors of the schools with ALA-accredited degrees soundly rejected the idea at a meeting between the leaders of the task force and the ALISE Council of Deans and Directors in 2002. The deans of leading information science schools, such as Michael Eisenberg of the University of Washington and Ray Von Dran of Syracuse University, spoke at length of their programs' affection for libraries and their commitment to library education. In her report to the executive board in 2002, the chair of the task force recommended abandonment of separate accreditation.[10]

The information science community, through the American Society for Information Science and Technology (ASIST), continues to consider, from time to time, whether a separate accreditation is feasible and appropriate.[11] In 2008, ASIST, with support from the Council of Library and Information Resources (CLIR), sponsored an invitational conference to discuss accrediting information science schools. Following a day of discussion, the conferees concluded that development of an accreditation process would be too problematic, in part because "Information professions are little recognized or understood by the general public and members of related disciplines."[12] There was a consensus that potential students have difficulty understanding what subject matter the information science programs actually address. Development of a separate accreditation seems unlikely because the iSchools do not want to bear the expense of an accrediting process and do not see sufficient benefits. It is possible that continued growth of iSchools, and in particular the growth of undergraduate information science programs, may lead to reconsideration of the idea. The IS undergraduate programs already in place could be joined by new ones or could expand their enrollment through distance learning, and their graduates would provide an alternative labor force for libraries, although many would seek opportunities in other employment sectors. Recognition of IS undergraduate degrees as legitimate credentials for entry-level librarians would go far to enhance the differences between librarianship and information science and to clarify the nature of each.

RECOGNITION OF BACHELOR'S DEGREES IN LIEU OF OR IN ADDITION TO MASTER'S DEGREES

While she was ALA president in 2006, Leslie Burger expressed hopes that a discussion of library education would consider some serious alternatives to the traditional MLS.[13] She asked whether MLS accreditation as it existed was worth the cost and whether baccalaureate education should be reconsidered. Others have floated the idea. At a conference of state librarians and library educators in 1999, I proposed a return to under-graduate library education as a solution to the shortage of librarians in the West, where there are few library schools. I said at that conference:

> When ALA and the profession fifty years ago defined "professional librar-ian" as one who holds an accredited master's degree, the reasons for doing so were to bring more learned people into the profession, to raise the status and salary of the profession, and to establish the professional credentials of librarians among other professions. It didn't work. After fifty years, it's time to reassess. Why do we believe that a mid-thirties person who hasn't been in school for years is a better candidate for library education than a twenty-year old who is familiar with contemporary technology and contemporary learning strategies? Why do we believe that entry-level librarianship is so complicated that a college graduate can't do it, but we do believe that college graduates can be software engineers, highway designers, editors, teachers, and accountants, just to name a few occupations that require only a bachelors degree? An undergraduate program would allow for better sequencing of courses and more hours in librarianship than most master's programs do. Undergraduate programs are cheaper for universities to administer—al-though they do bring in less revenue than graduate programs do.[14]

The key portion of the argument I made then is that an undergraduate program would provide more courses in library science, which could be offered in increasing complexity in sequenced structures.

The principle for shifting library education to the bachelor's degree is that level and structure of an educational program for an occupation ought to be based on the work its graduates will do: form should follow function. There are practical advantages to moving professional educa-tion to the bachelor's level. The conditions that led the profession to abandon bachelor's degrees as professional credentials in 1950 no longer exist. Several difficulties of the existing system would be overcome by returning to undergraduate programs in librarianship and by consider-ing bachelor's degrees as first professional degrees. The arguments for a return to the BS degree are similar to the arguments Anita Hostetter made in the 1940s. Bachelor's degree programs would allow for more courses in library science than the twelve courses now generally taken in MLS programs. They would allow for more sequenced courses so that not ev-ery course taken would be an introduction to a topic. They would reduce the cost of preparation for a career and perhaps attract a different kind of student than we now have. If persons were prepared for the profession at younger ages and in shorter programs of study (a total of 4–6 years in-stead of 6–9 years), they could have longer careers and more opportunities to develop and advance as professionals. Undergraduate majors in library science could be coordinated with the growing number of library technician programs in the community colleges. If librarians had longer careers and shorter preparation times, there could be more stability in the supply of librarians. Master's degree programs would build on the knowledge acquired in undergraduate programs and could include more sophisticated content than is now possible.

Those universities that want to do so could continue to offer master's degrees as entry-level credentials for persons who had other undergraduate degrees through practitioner master's degrees similar to the master of arts in teaching degree that is commonly available for teachers. Costs would be lower for both students and universities (here I refer to the cost to host universities, not to the library education programs). The cost to students is but a portion of the whole cost of educating a class of librarians, because tuition and fees cover only a small portion of the cost of education. It is possible that the costs of operating library schools would be the same at whatever level degrees are offered, but it seems likely that if library education were moved back to the undergraduate level, the cost to society of supporting those programs eventually would be less. Students who currently major in other undergraduate programs would shift to library science majors, but the universities would not have the burden of maintaining graduate programs.

The advantages presented in the preceding discussion are confronted by the disadvantage that the proposal is anathema to so many. The library schools, who would have to lead the effort both within librarianship and on their own campuses, would feel their stature threatened by such a move, and there is too much distrust and competition among the schools to imagine them making a concerted effort. Returning to the BS would call for major revamping of the ALA Office of Accreditation and the ALA Committee on Accreditation if the schools that offered the degree sought accreditation. However, there is no reason that undergraduate degrees would have to have ALA accreditation unless those who hire librarians continue to insist that new hires have degrees from accredited schools. A return to bachelor's degrees would also call for the ALA to alter its policy on human resource utilization, which is honored in the breach more than in practice. The ALA might also reconsider the initiatives it has begun through the Allied Professional Association that are designed to certify individuals as second-class librarians (certified paraprofessionals). Such changes are unlikely in a large organization whose policies are shaped at least as much by its professional staff as by its members. The ALA is a conservative organization that operates much like a large corporation, moved, when it moves, by its officers and staff, not by its members or shareholders.[15]

The many ALA members who have accredited master's degrees and value the distinction those degrees mark between them and "nonprofessionals" are unlikely to support such a move. Richard Dougherty no doubt spoke for many when, in a 2007 Web seminar, he responded to a participant's suggestion that the bachelor's degree be reestablished as a professional credential by saying that such a move would have a negative impact on librarians' salaries and status. He repeated the same arguments made in 1948, that librarianship would be less professional if bachelor's degrees were available because people would seek shorter routes to employment, and that libraries would employ lesser credentialed people to cut costs.[16] In other words, Dougherty fears that without a rule to force them to do it, neither libraries nor potential librarians would invest in the MLS. The origin and continuation of the MLS project is an example of how a practice can be created and enforced by a professional association, in this case the ALA, and of how a practice is perpetuated because those who have followed it cannot imagine that others should not be required to follow it also.

EXPANDED DEVELOPMENT
OF MULTIPLE MODELS TO TRAIN LIBRARIANS

There already are a variety of ways to acquire the skills needed to work as a librarian. These models are based on a functional concept of professionalism and are grounded in the realities of present situations. They deal with the immediate need for training for the actual practice of librarianship, outside the rubric of the MLS.

The most outstanding example of another model lies in school librarianship. School librarians are the largest group of librarians. Only some school librarians are required to have an ALA-accredited MLS to practice their profession. The states and the school districts make the rules for school librarians. They require certification, and they define it in myriad ways.[17] Whatever librarians' path is to certification, the students and teachers recognize them as their school librarians by virtue of their functions in the school.

Alternative certification is one of these paths. It presents a good example of a different possibility for education of librarians who work in nonschool settings. There are two recent alternative certification projects in Texas, where to be a school librarian one must have teaching experience and a master's degree (it does not matter in what subject), and one must pass a state test. To take the test, a person must be "recommended" by a state-recognized agency. The movement for accountability and effectiveness that one sees in higher education also motivates policy and practice in the K–12 school world. The agencies that may recommend librarians for state testing now include universities, school districts, private companies whose business is test preparation, and regional service centers. What is important to the state is not which kind of institution one attended but whether one succeeds on the test. The recommending agencies of whatever type are held accountable, in terms of continuing authority to recommend students, based on the test scores of those they recommend. The Institute of Museum and Library Services (IMLS) has funded partnerships between universities and these other various agencies to prepare teachers to become school librarians, but the recommending agency need not be a university. In 2005, the IMLS funded Alternative Preparation for Librarians in Urban Schools (A-PLUS), a collaborative project between Texas Woman's University School of Library and Information Studies and the Dallas Independent School District's Alternative Certification Program. In A-PLUS, students receive intensive training in a summer program, then continue their education while being employed full time as school librarians. In 2009, the IMLS funded a similar program at Sam Houston State University, working in partnership with school districts and state regional service centers. These alternative paths to certification create real librarians who learn and work simultaneously. The whole profession will have to extend to them the same recognition that is extended to traditionally prepared librarians.

Alternative certification is an important development in the history of education for librarianship. It is a harbinger of new institutional arrangements and partnerships and responsibilities. Because it is a certification program, it demonstrates the feasibility of individual certification. It is also a harbinger of new opportunities for individuals to acquire the knowledge they need to practice a profession while they are working in it.

Another harbinger is a coalition within traditional library education, Web-based Information Science Education (WISE), an international consortium of fifteen schools.[18] In the WISE program, schools offer online courses through which students at any member institution may earn credits with assurance of transfer of credits. WISE could be a precursor to a system in which students register for library education classes from a variety of schools' curricula to compile a portfolio of courses. That portfolio could then be recognized by the ALA, by some licensing agency, or by an individual school through relaxation of barriers such as limited transfer of courses.

Another model already in use, one that could be enhanced by drawing on elements of alternative certification and consortium-based distance learning, relates to education of directors and staff of small public libraries. The patrons of small community libraries recognize the people who work there as librarians because of the role they play. State libraries recognize the need to support these public librarians. In states such as Texas and Illinois, the state libraries offer training programs designed for library practitioners in small public libraries. The IMLS has funded some of these programs, recognizing a real need that cannot be addressed feasibly through the conventional MLS model. An example of a collaborative model that uses a variety of education providers is the Continuum of Library Education Project, originally funded by the IMLS through a grant to the Council of Western State Librarians. The purpose of the project was to develop a certification program for "library practitioners," defined as public library directors or managers who do not have MLS degrees. The Continuum project was funded to develop a standard certification program for library practitioners in the Western states; a set of competencies was seen as a prerequisite to a certification program. The Continuum project developed and validated a list of competencies and a standard certification process for the Western states.[19] The set of competencies developed for these library practitioners comprises many skills that are equal to or exceed the skills of graduates of MLS programs. In the process of developing the lists, library practitioners made it clear that they believe themselves to be true librarians, even though they do not hold MLS degrees.[20]

The programs of the ALA Allied Professional Association (APA) suggest other models. The APA was created as a companion organization to the ALA, "to promote the mutual professional interests of librarians and other library workers."[21] Some APA activities are directed toward continuing education of librarians as defined by the ALA. Other programs, however, are directed toward "other library workers." In 2009, the APA announced the creation of the Library Support Staff Certification Program (LSSCP), funded by the IMLS.[22] Those who complete the program will be certified to have competencies that are appropriate to the roles of support staff. Programs that standardize the skill sets for these librarians could be beneficial to employees and employers alike. A danger inherent in the LSSCP, and indeed in the existence of APA, is that it risks cementing the concept that there are "professional librarians" and "others." The creation of competency statements for support staff risks formalizing their skills limitations, to show that support staff certifiably have limited abilities compared to MLS librarians. While the ALA competency statements adopted in 2009 lack sufficient detail to make explicit comparisons to other competency lists, many of the ALA divisions have more detailed competency lists, so it will be interesting to see how the LSSCP lists will compare to those. Library support staff, or library technicians, play important roles in libraries. These "other workers" are 60 percent of the library workforce. However, if the outcome is to certify them as "other" than true librarians, the project risks solidifying invidious, nonfunctional distinctions among library workers.

There are more radical possibilities. One is to abandon accreditation altogether. It is difficult to imagine the ALA taking that step, so it would have to be the result of a mass secession from the process by the library schools, and that seems unlikely. Over the years, various school deans have threatened to withdraw, but the few that did only did so because they were prepared to give up library education, as at the University of California, Berkeley. Other professional schools thrive without an accreditation process, or with one that is optional and not a matter of programmatic survival, such as schools of journalism and teacher education.

Some other possibilities include shifting validation of educational credentials from a focus on individual library education programs to a focus on individual portfolios and credentials, such as replacement of accredited degrees with licensure for individuals. The certification programs for library practitioners and library technicians described above join the long-standing certification programs for school librarians as examples of approaches that meet the public demand for accountability. Certification of individual librarians, using the school librarian model, is based on demonstration of an individual's competence; the set of competencies an individual must demonstrate are related to the needs of clients. Individual certification, as opposed to specialized accreditation, would make librarianship more like the higher-status professions. All of librarianship has much to learn from the certification models in school librarianship. Another possibility is to offer library education through the ALA and its divisions, either bypassing or contracting with the library schools.[23]

Without formal announcements or actions, the libraries could abandon or ignore a standard credentialing system for staff and assume responsibility for their services and outcomes using whatever personnel resources each deems most suitable to its purposes. The latter is already the approach implied in both institutional and specialized accreditation standards, such as those of the Southern Association of Colleges and Schools and the American Veterinary Medical Association.[24] It is the practice in many school libraries and it is what the diverse set of libraries referred to as "special libraries" have long done. Except for librarians who chose to acknowledge and follow them, the ALA's policies on education have been largely irrelevant to sponsors, funders, hosts, and even many library administrations. The 1970 policy "Library Education and Manpower," renamed "Library Education and Personnel Utilization" in 1976, and the current "Library and Information Studies and Human Resource Utilization" adopted in 2002 have been inconsistently enforced work rules. As a practical matter, libraries use whatever personnel resources they deem most suitable to their purposes at costs they can afford. Libraries are accountable to their sponsors (schools, cities, universities) for providing services and positive outcomes. The libraries' responsibilities to carry out their functions continue whether ALA-credentialed staff are available or not. To fulfill their roles, libraries may redefine positions so that nonlibrarians perform tasks once carried out by librarians, or especially in the case of adapting to new technologies, they may hire persons to work as librarians whose educational and experience credentials are in another profession. In times of shortages of librarians, such as the late 1990s, or shortages of funds for positions, as in the current recession, or in times of rapid technological change (especially since the advent of the browsable Internet in 1992), libraries have met their personnel needs by turning to the labor force available at prices they can afford. There is a labor market.

Changes in the social environments and contexts are more likely to be the forces for change than are ALA actions, particularly if the ALA waits on the Committee on Accreditation for leadership. The processes of change may vary by type of library. The changes in the circumstances in which librarians work have begun to impel a change in personnel practices. While it may be some time before these personnel changes are acknowledged in the elaborate way that the MLS project has been acknowledged, they are nonetheless important changes. Library directors are discovering that the expertise they need is not found only in graduates of library schools, particularly in relation to technology. These incremental changes may eventually lead to explicit, widespread recognition that the accredited MLS is only one professional degree appropriate for the variety of professional skills that are needed to operate contemporary libraries. The discriminatory phrase "support staff" might even be purged from librarians' vocabularies. In public librarianship, while many library directors and library boards will continue to insist that new professional librarians hold accredited master's degrees, others, even some who pay lip service to the MLS project, will redefine staff positions so that they can hire individuals with other educational credentials and expertise as needed.

As library staffs begin to include more people whose training is in fields other than librarianship, it seems likely that some of them will voice dissatisfaction at not being considered real professionals, and eventually a new situation will evolve in which they will have substantial power and will make decisions based on their agenda. A similar process is already under way in academic libraries. In academe, the role of traditional faculty and traditional staff, such as librarians, is increasingly challenged by new kinds of academic professionals, holding a wide variety of types and levels of degrees, who want to assert their claims to status and power within colleges and universities. Technology specialists, distance learning specialists, academic support professionals, and institutional effectiveness officers all make claims on professionalism and its associated academic rights and privileges. New policies on the academic status of these new professionals may call into question the comparability of credentials and rewards.

TOWARD CHANGE

Each option described above rests on its own principle, but the principle underlying the general proposition that there should be multiple models for preparation for library work is simply this: organizations and institutions that survive are those that adapt to circumstances rather than attempting to force their will on the world. Perhaps a disadvantage of adopting a flexible stance toward credentials for librarians is that it leads away from a standardized definition of "librarian" and away from efforts to develop a science or theory of libraries. But those efforts have not gone well anyway. Library administrators would find themselves living with a degree of risk and uncertainty. The advantage of this approach to the situation is that it does not call for a confrontation with or an intervention by the ALA or library schools; it does not call for profession-wide management or concerted action, but for initiative and enterprise among those who hire and develop librarians.

The community of librarians and the communities librarians serve have some choices. There are many alternatives, some of which are described above. The evidence suggests that it is time to abandon the MLS project and develop a new scheme for library education. Reader surveys (which included professional librarians and support staff) conducted by *Library Journal* in 1994 and 2007 showed that about 70 percent of those polled who work in libraries believe the MLS is important to their work—but nearly a third do not.[25]

Library education may continue on its present path, despite its inherent difficulties. The MLS, renamed the MLIS, may live on to an old age, battered and criticized, perhaps a bit demented, but enduring. There are reasons to think so. The various congresses and committees and task forces that the ALA has commissioned have not produced fresh visions but have focused on old squabbles, such as the difference between information science and library science, on practice versus theory, or on the internal operations of the schools, as if the ALA could force universities to operate in particular ways. Evidence about events or options in the various ALA task force reports has been limited or nonexistent. Instead, decisions have been based on opinions expressed. There is no organized voice for change. Many librarians would feel threatened by seeing a new degree, perhaps at a lower level, such as a bachelor of science degree, treated as an employment credential equal to their master's degrees.

The library educators' association, ALISE, is not a voice for reform. Like its predecessor association, the AALS, ALISE has had little influence in library school development. Its membership has been declining for years. It has no role in the accrediting process, which operates through the ALA. As one critic, Donald Gordon Davis, said of the AASL in 1974, "the main impetus for continued existence seemed to come from a simple desire for association or fellowship." In what seems to be true of ALISE as well, Davis wrote of the AASL: "because of close ties of the faculties to various subgroups of the practitioner association, which were apparently deemed more rewarding and prestigious, a strong identity of the school association failed to emerge."[26]

Davis's conclusion was seconded by William Summers in 1986.[27] Summers saw hopes for growth, but in fact membership continued to decline, particularly among new faculty, and the association became increasingly peripheral to professional education policy.[28] Library educators have played strong roles in the Committee on Accreditation, but ALISE has not been a major player in accreditation.

Higher education and professional librarianship both are conservative institutions. Radical change appeals to neither. Both focus their energies on preserving their professional domains. They respond to challenges and to new situations by seeking to make dissidents, critics, or possible new collaborators conform to their traditional practices and perspectives. Librarianship and higher education are comfortable together. Universities like graduate programs, particularly those that operate at low costs. Librarianship likes its graduate degrees and accreditation. Presently, neither is possible without universities. While universities could live without library schools, only a small number have chosen to close them.

Still, change has happened before. However unlikely it may seem that American librarians will give up the MLS, we should remember Joseph Wheeler's comment about the possibility of starting the project in 1946. Commenting on the problems of moving from the existing situation to a new model, he wrote, the "difficulty seems insurmountable."[29] Yet merely five years later, the MLS project was underway. There are signs that change is possible: the perennial complaints about relevance of graduate library education are as loud as ever; there is governmental and regulatory pressure to shorten degree programs; public and legislative doubts about the quality of some graduate degree programs in similar fields such as education are voiced regularly; and the 2008 federal Higher Education Act and new regional accreditation standards pressure universities to demonstrate the efficiency and effectiveness of their programs. The most important sign that change may be possible, or even necessary, is the transition from the use of print in libraries as an information resource to the use of electronic information retrieved from the Internet. Libraries may be the place where that access happens insofar as they offer connected computers to people who do not have their own and libraries have licenses for collective access to proprietary databases, but the implications for the continued need for graduate training are ominous.

The MLS project was adopted at a historical moment when librarianship seemed stable, in the sense that what the profession needed, and what libraries needed, was more of the same, not something different. Libraries needed more staff, more books, more buildings. Librarians needed more in their salaries and more prestige. In the present historical moment, libraries and librarians still need "more" of those things. But it is more apparent now than it was in 1950 that libraries and those they serve also need different resources. Technology has wrought revolutionary changes in the ways knowledge records are created, distributed, used, and preserved. Technological change is intertwined with social changes that challenge traditional concepts and the institutions such as libraries that formalize them into action programs.

The appropriate content and structure of education for librarianship ideally would be designed based on an understanding of the nature and roles of libraries, but that future is uncertain, and it likely always will be. Whether types of libraries will become more or less similar to one another is an open question, as are whether a meaningful distinction can be maintained between "support" and "professional" work and whether librarians should continue to be consumers of technology or should engage in technology design, just to name a few big questions. These big questions will not have immediate or easy answers. What seems clear is that the library education system will contribute to these answers if it is focused on addressing social purposes through solutions that change as needs and tools change. It also seems clear that library functions that are responsive to change will call for more expertise, both technological and social, and that an education system to provide appropriately skilled librarians will require more time and structure than the present system offers. As answers to the big questions evolve, a system of education of librarians will require flexibility so that educational programs can participate productively in shaping answers and in shaping new librarians.

The shift in society toward stress on the outcomes, performance, and value-adding capability of institutions will contribute to a change in views of traditional institutions, like libraries. Those views have been based on belief in these institutions' inherent good and cultural authority. Libraries still are associated with books.[30] That link in the popular mind gave libraries cultural authority when books had cultural authority. But as books are augmented by new technologies as sources of wisdom and credibility, and as other institutions, physical or virtual, acquire their own privileged positions as valid conveyors of knowledge and authority, libraries may lose the special place they have held as temples of culture.

Americans, even those who do not use them, respect and value libraries because they believe libraries are important agencies. Society recognizes that libraries' central role as vehicles for sharing resources has benefits for individuals and for whole groups. While librarians may not enjoy as positive an image in the public mind as librarians would like to have, the same could be said of most occupations. The quest for status and prestige and other rewards through the MLS has had at least as many negative consequences as positive ones. The negative consequences are almost all for those who work in libraries: a caste structure, an expensive education, and consumption of enormous human capital in debating and tinkering with education for the job. Librarians' efforts to build their status and prestige have done substantial harm to their own partners, the library practitioners who work in libraries, often doing the same tasks as "professional" librarians but without the rewards and recognition.

Acknowledging that the MLS project did not accomplish its goals should not be seen as a negative conclusion. Rather, a sentiment heard in professional sports seems appropriate: "It is what it is."[31] If the MLS project had succeeded, one might say, "Here is a model to extend to other cases." But, as in the case of all assessments of projects that fail, it is reasonable to say, "We tried that and it didn't work, so we should now try something different." Self-aware people can question the reasons for their own actions and can ask themselves why they might believe some options are unthinkable. In the process, they may discover that some things that were unthinkable turn out to be pretty good ideas.

After more than fifty years of disappointment, librarians may recognize that the situation calls for a serious discussion, informed by evidence and not just hopes, of what a different direction could be and what models for professional education could serve as complements or replacements to the MLS. Librarians could look at their situation objectively. They could accept that they have been prisoners, not beneficiaries. They could seek to understand which efforts are productive and which are not. Librarians could seek different ways to make their own lives and careers better, and new structures to form the careers of the next generation of librarians. The result could be better service to the people who depend on the professionalism of librarians.

NOTES

1. Samuel Haber, *The Quest for Authority and Honor in the American Professions, 1750–1900* (Chicago: University of Chicago Press, 1991), 204.

2. Louis Shores, "The Education of an American Librarian," 1953, in *Mark Hopkins' Log and Other Essays by Louis Shores*, selected by John David Marshall (Hamden, Conn.: Shoe String, 1965), 49, 243.

3. For example, see Leigh Estabrook, "Labor and Librarians: The Divisiveness of Professionalism," *Library Journal*, January 15, 1981, 125–7; William F. Birdsall, "Librarianship, Professionalism, and Social Change," *Library Journal*, February 1, 1982, 223–6.

4. George A. Kelly, *A Theory of Personality: The Psychology of Personal Constructs* (New York: Norton, 1963).

5. ALA Library Fact Sheet No. 2, www.ala.org.

6. William K. Selden, *Accreditation: A Struggle over Standards in Higher Education* (New York: Harper and Brothers, 1960), 6.

7. American Library Association Committee on Accreditation, "COA Response to the Final Report of the Presidential Task Force on Library Education, June 1, 2009," www.ala.org.

8. "COA Response to the Final Report of the Presidential Task Force on Library Education."

9. "Professional Education Task Forces Established," *Prism* 8, no. 1 (2000): 1.

10. American Library Association Executive Board, midwinter 2002, www.ala.org.

11. American Society for Information Science and Technology, "ASIS&T Issues Study on Graduate Information Programs and Accreditation," 2008, www.asis.org.

12. ASIST, "Information Professions Accreditation Meeting, September 9, 2008, Meeting Report, Information Professionals Task Force," www.asis.org.

13. Leslie Burger, "ALA's Alternative to an MLS," *Library Journal*, November 1, 2006, 10.

14. Keith Swigger, "The Shortage of Librarians," remarks prepared for Western Conference of State Librarians, Carefree, Arizona, December 8, 1999.

15. John E. Buschman, *Dismantling the Public Sphere: Situating and Sustaining Librarianship in the Age of the New Public Philosophy* (Westport, Conn.: Libraries Unlimited, 2003), chap. 7.

16. "Library Education: Facing New Realities," Webcast April 27, 2007, Web seminar sponsored by College of DuPage, Glen Ellyn, Illinois.

17. Elizabeth A. Kaye and Jeffrey J. Makos, *Requirements for Certification of Teachers, Counselors, Librarians, Administrators for Elementary and Secondary Schools, 2008–2009* (Chicago: University of Chicago Press, 2008) (published annually since 1935).

18. Web-based Information Science Education, "About WISE," www.ala.org.

19. "Library Practitioner Certificate Program, Western Council of State Libraries," http://certificate.westernco.org.

20. Catherine Helmick and Keith Swigger, "Core Competencies of Library Practitioners," *Public Libraries* 45, no. 2 (2006): 55–76.

21. ALA Allied Professional Association, www.ala-apa.org.

22. ALA-APA News Release, "ALA Announces Approval of Library Support Staff Certification (LSSC), July 21, 2009," www.ala.org.

23. Keith Swigger, "Education for an Ancient Profession in the Twenty-first Century," in *Change and Continuity in Librarianship: Approaching the Twenty-first Century: Proceedings of the 40th Military Librarians Workshop*, ed. Richard Werking (Annapolis, Md.: U.S. Naval Academy, 1998).

24. Southern Association of Colleges and Schools, www.sacscoc.org; American Veterinary Medical Association, www.avma.org.

25. Evan St. Lifer, "Are You Happy in Your Job?" *Library Journal*, November 1, 1994, 44–49; John N. Berry, "Great Work, Genuine Problems," *Library Journal*, October 1, 2007, 26–29.

26. Donald Gordon Davis Jr., *The Association of American Library Schools, 1915–1968* (Metuchen, N.J.: Scarecrow, 1974), 299, 301.

27. F. William Summers, "Role of the Association for Library and Information Science Education in Library and Information Science Education," *Library Trends* 34, no. 4 (1986): 667–77.

28. Gretchen Whitney, "Library and Information Science Educators: Membership Trends in the Association for Library and Information Science Education, 1986–87 to 1996–97," *Journal of Education for Library and Information Science* 39, no. 1 (1998): 38–57.

29. Joseph L. Wheeler, *Progress and Problems in Education for Librarianship* (New York: Carnegie Corporation, 1946), 26.

30. Cathy De Rosa, *Perceptions of Libraries and Information Resources: A Report to the OCLC Membership* (Dublin, Ohio: OCLC, 2005).

31. William Safire, "It Is What It Is," *New York Times*, March 5, 2006.

Index

IMLS (Institute of Museum and Library Services), 81, 98, 144–45
income. *See* salaries
individual certification, 146
information literacy, 100
"Information Power," 99
information profession, 23–24, 121–24
information science, 5–6, 77–80, 139–40
information technologies: academic librarians and, 95; computer-related occupations compared to librarianship, 30, *31, 43,* 44; expertise for new positions, 147–48; impact on library education alternatives, 149–51; knowledge workers, 101–3; librarians as users, not designers, of, 96
"innovators," 70
institutions: accreditation of, 8–9; affecting librarians' work, 99–101, 113–14; made as needed, 128; professional associations' relationships with, 112–13
intellectual base for librarianship, 15
iSchools Caucus, 78, 83, 120, 140

job market. *See* employment of librarians; shortages of librarians
jurisdiction model of professionalism, 121–24

Kelly, George, 136
King Report, 45
knowledge types, 116–18
knowledge workers' challenge, 101–3

Lancaster, F. W., 113
Larson, Magali, 118, 120–21
law, librarianship compared to, 117
Learning4Life plan, 99–100
Leigh, Robert, 12, 32, 51, 69–70, 80, 81
liberal arts education, 59–61, *61,* 83–84
librarian, defining, 2, 90. *See also* professionalism
libraries as nonessential institutions, 119–20
library and information science, 5–6

"Library and Information Studies and Human Resource Utilization," 146
"Library and Information Studies and Human Resource Utilization Policy Statement," 91–92
library assistants: differentiation between professional librarians and, 15; prestige comparisons, 30; salary comparisons, 33–34, 97; shortages of librarians impacting, *43,* 43–44; status of, 28, 97
"Library Education and Manpower," 90–92, 146
"Library Education and Personnel Utilization," 146
Library Journal reader survey, 148
"Library Manpower Needs and Utilization," 90
library practitioners program, 144–45
library schools: closings, 80, 136; core areas of study, 70; curriculum moving to graduate level, 13–14, 69–70; faculty, 81–83, *82;* grade inflation, 56; graduates, *39–40,* 40–42, *42,* 86; status of, 82–83; students, 51–54, *53,* 56 *See also* enrollment in library school
Library Services Act, 38
Library Support Staff Certification Program (LSSCP), 145–46
library technician programs, 98
licensure for individuals, 146
Lieberman, Jethro, 126
Lincecum, Taylor, 70
Lorenzen, Michael, 113–14
Lounsbury, John W., 50–51
LSSCP (Library Support Staff Certification Program), 145–46
Lynch, Beverly, 4

Macklin, David B., 57–59, *58*
male librarians, 112
manual labor, 122–23
Markey, Karen, 70
Martin, Lowell, 14
Master of Library and Information Science (MLIS), 5–6

master's degree in library science (MLS): affecting age of library school students, 57; costs of, 84–86, *85*; enrollment and graduation data, 38, *39–40*, 40–42, *42*; MLIS variation, 5–6; percentage of librarians with, 45–46; recognition of, 89–96; two-year advanced degree eliminated by, 68

master's degree types, 67–68

Miller, Wharton, 17–18

Mishoff, Willard, 46

MLIS (Master of Library and Information Science), 5–6

Moen, William E., 52, 62

Munn, Ralph, 17

Nam, Charles, 25–26

Nam-Powers score, 31–32

National Center for Educational Statistics (NCES), 38

National Council of Accreditation for Teacher Education (NCATE), 94

National Opinion Research Center (NORC), 24, 30, 127–28

NCATE (National Council of Accreditation for Teacher Education), 94

NCES (National Center for Educational Statistics), 38

Neal, James, 95

Nelson, Bonnie, 77, 127

nonessential institutions, 119–20

nonprofessional work, 12

NORC (National Opinion Research Center), 24, 30, 127–28

normative knowledge, 117–18

occupational associations, 125–26. *See also* American Library Association (ALA)

occupational comparisons: data reporting, 45; peer professions, 23–24; of prestige, 47, *47–48*; of status, 26–28; workforce growth, *43*, 43–44

Office of Accreditation, 142–43

Office of Research and Statistics, 59

options for library education: abandonment of accreditation, 146; alternative backgrounds without MLS, 146–48; bachelor degrees, 140–43; continuation of present system, 137–39; creation of new accrediting agencies, 139–40; multiple models, 143–48; need for, 148–51

organizational professions, 101, 114

outcomes assessment, 4–5, 74

Park, Chung I., 113

part-time faculty in library schools, 81–83, *82*

patrons. *See* public perceptions

Pemberton, Anne E., 50–51

personality traits. *See* image

personnel, alternative, 146–48

power model of professionalism, 118–21

Powers, Mary, 26

Presidential Task Force on Library Education, 139

prestige: compared to status, 25; desire for, 15, 20; Harris poll, 24; students' views of, 47, *47–48*; studies of, 30, *31*

professional accreditation, 8–9

professionalism: alternative approach to, 127–29; claiming, 114–15; as flawed construct, 126–27; jurisdiction model, 121–24; power model, 118–21; as relationship, 127; as symbol, 124–26; trait model, 109–18, 122–23, 126; values/factual question of, 107–8

professional master's degrees, 68

Progress and Problems in Education for Librarianship, 16–17

public librarians, 23, 92–93, 98

Public Library Association (PLA), 100–101

Public Library Inquiry, 11–12, 45, 48, 51, 62, 70, 89

The Public Library in the United States, 12–13

About the Author

Keith Swigger is professor in the School of Library and Information Studies at Texas Woman's University, where he has been a member of the faculty since 1981 and served as dean of the Library and Information Studies (1991–2000) and Professional Education (2000–2003) programs. He holds an AB in history from the University of Chicago and an MA from the Graduate Library School, an MA in history from Indiana University, and a PhD in American civilization from the University of Iowa. He taught and served as a librarian at the University of Iowa and taught in the interdisciplinary New Center for Learning at East Texas State University. He has written and spoken frequently about education for librarianship and has played a role in creating innovative programs in distance learning and alternative certification. His teaching responsibilities include courses in information professions, academic librarianship, and management.

UNIVERSITY OF MAINE AT AUGUSTA

3 2304 00093137 6

JAN 11 2011